THE WIT AND WISDOM *of BILLY GRAHAM*

THE WIT AND WISDOM *of BILLY GRAHAM*

EDITED AND COMPILED
by BILL ADLER

RANDOM HOUSE NEW YORK

First Printing

Published in New York by Random House, Inc., and simultaneously
in Toronto, Canada, by Random House of Canada Limited.

Library of Congress Catalog Card Number: 66-21481

Manufactured in the United States of America
by H. Wolff, New York.
Designed by Carl Weiss

TABLE of CONTENTS

One of Billy Graham's most effective means of communicating his ideas is through parables such as the following:

I heard the story of a man who walked along a road, tired, weary, and discouraged. He could hardly put one foot ahead of the other. A neighbor overtook him in a wagon and invited him to ride with him. As they rode along together his neighbor noticed that the tired, weary man still carried a heavy sack of grain on his back.

"Put that down," he said, "you don't need to carry that."

The tired man said, "Oh, it's enough for you to carry me, let alone this sack of grain."

There are thousands of you who have turned to God, but you are still carrying your burdens. But God begs of you: "Cast all your care on Me, for I care for you."

"The Cure for Discouragement"
The Hour of Decision, 1954

INTRODUCTION

For almost two decades William Franklin Graham has brought the "good news" of the gospel to listeners of all faiths throughout the world. By means of extensive personal crusades, and with the aid of a weekly radio broadcast, *The Hour of Decision*—and by hourly television programs from his crusades to several hundred cities in the United States and Canada—he has brought comfort and guidance to millions of the faithful, and has won thousands more over to a Christian life. His voice rings like that of an irrepressible conscience in the ear of a nation that seems to have abandoned the moral principles of its founders. He remains an uncompromising critic of sin, hypocrisy, injustice, and moral lethargy wherever they exist in today's society. And he has consistently offered a single solution to all of the many ills besetting mankind—salvation through Jesus Christ.

The evangelism of Billy Graham, an ordained Southern Baptist minister, is in the American tradition of Billy Sunday and others who have preached "hot Hell and freezing snow" to revival meetings for over a century. But Billy Graham has also brought to his evangelism a new degree of intellectualism, in conscious reaction to the sometimes rabid emotionalism of his predecessors. By his own admission, emotional appeal can be a dramatic device at revivals but has little lasting effect upon the supposed "converts." He believes that true conversion involves more than emotional response; the true Christian must make an active, intelligent commitment of the will. Rather than retreating into the sanctuary of religious obscurantism, Billy Graham has attempted to meet intellectual critics of Christianity on their own terms.

Billy Graham is also a man with a keen sense of humor. Indeed, a good sense of humor and a ready wit are indispensable assets to a public figure of his stature. His sermons abound with anecdotes, tall tales, pointed parables, and just plain jokes, all of which often have the double virtue of being both diverting and enlightening.

This book, compiled from sermons, speeches, and interviews over Billy Graham's entire career, records in his own words the great evangelist's thoughts and feelings on today's most significant issues. His discussions range from personal behavior to international politics, including morality in the home, teen-age problems, civil rights, and the Cold War. They are of vital concern to everyone. What emerges from these words is a self-portrait by a most fascinating individual—Billy Graham, a modern man of God.

Bill Adler
New York City

THE WIT AND WISDOM *of BILLY GRAHAM*

CHAPTER I:

GOD, MAN, AND RELIGION

Billy Graham discusses the nature of God and His relation to man:

The Bible says God Almighty created the human race for a special purpose. God is love. He wanted some other creatures in the universe like Himself, made in His image, little gods who had a will of their own who could return love to Him.

God was lovely; God craved and wanted fellowship. Incredible as that sounds, God wanted fellowship.

He wanted somebody to love Him and He created the human race and put them on this planet. He said if you will obey the moral laws of the universe, we will walk together and build a wonderful and beautiful world together. But if you rebel against this, if you break the moral laws, you will suffer and die and be judged.

"Why God Allows Suffering and War"
Houston Crusade, 1965

A starving man's chief interest is food. A thirsty man's chief interest is water. A wounded man's chief interest is a physician. And a lost man's chief need, whether he realizes it or not, is God.

"The Cure for Anxiety"
The Hour of Decision, 1957

The trouble with our modern thinking is that we have a conception that God is a haphazard God with no set rules of life and salvation.

Ask the astronomer if God is a haphazard God. He will tell you that every star moves with precision in its celestial path. To ignore the rules of the universe would spell ruin to that star. To deviate from its God-ordained course would mean tragedy and deterioration.

Ask the scientist if God is a haphazard God. He will tell you that his formulas and equations are fixed and that to ignore the laws of science would be a fool's folly. If the laws in the material realm are so fixed and exact, is it reasonable that God could afford to be haphazard in the spiritual realm where eternal destinies of souls are at stake? I say no, a thousand times no!

Just as God had equations and rules in the material realm, God has equations and rules in the spiritual. The Bible says, "The wages of sin, is death" (Romans 6:23). That is God's formula; and when a man sins, he is going to pay for it in this life and the life to come. That is just as certain as two plus two equals four.

"The Signs of the Times"
The Hour of Decision, 1957

Billy Graham relates the existence of apparent deformity and illness to the nature of God:

God is especially close to us when we are lying on a sickbed. God will make the bed soft and will freshen it with his presence and with his tender care. He makes the bed comfortable and wipes away our tears. He ministers to us with special tenderness at such a time and reveals His great love for us.

Tell me why the gardener trims and prunes his rosebushes, sometimes cutting away productive branches with both hands, and I will tell you why God's people are afflicted. God's hand never slips. He never makes a mistake. His every move is for our good and for our ultimate good. Oftentimes He must deform us and mutilate our own image. Deformity sometimes precedes conformity. The knowledge of this caused Paul to sing, "Most gladly therefore will I rather glory in my infirmities, that the power of Christ may rest upon me."

"Clouds"
The Hour of Decision, 1960

Billy Graham deals with the notion that "God is on our side":

We have an idea in this country that God is changed to accommodate Himself for Americans. We have an idea that we Americans are God's chosen people, and God loves us more than any other people and that we are God's blessed.

I tell you that God doesn't love us any more than He does the Russians. He doesn't love us any more than he does the Chinese. He doesn't love us any more than he does the Africans. God doesn't love us any more than any other people.

Opening Sermon
Charlotte Crusade, 1958

Although Billy Graham's assessment of the nature of man is not very bright, it is by no means hopeless:

What exactly is the nature of man, who is capable of the atrocities accompanying the extermination of the Jews and capable of bestiality such as practiced by Mau-Mau? The most savage animal is incapable of sinking to the depths which the Eichmann trial revealed. This trial makes the humanist sound ridiculous when he talks about man's capacity to realize all his potentialities. Man may be progressing in many areas, but he still betrays his moral degeneracy at times like these. The Roman game of throwing Christians to the lions was a side show in comparison to what was unveiled in the Eichmann trial.

What happens when a society with a history of learning and culture like that of Germany sinks so low? The Bible gives the answer when it says, "The heart is deceitful above all things, and desperately wicked: who can know it?" (Jeremiah 17:9). Even those who point with self-righteousness either to Mau-Mau, Nazism, or any other cruel barbarism also have deceitful hearts. You do not ever know your own heart, nor the depths to which it will sink under certain circumstances. What was revealed in the Eichmann trail is man's sinful nature pushing through this veneer of social culture.

Primitive forces are exhibited in the most civilized nations. It is known that the Mau-Mau oaths and ceremonies were conceived by the more educated of the Kikuyu Tribe in East Africa. They played upon the superstitions of the still very primitive people. So bestial and disgusting are the ceremonies that it is doubtful if uneducated minds could have thought of them. These modern illustrations indicate that man is anything but the good person the humanist would like to think he is. Quite the contrary, they confirm the Biblical diagnosis of man.

Man is born with a sinful nature, and unless it is transformed by the power of God, it is capable of indescribable brutality and evil. And yet no man needs to be controlled by these natural forces of wickedness, for the power of God through the Gospel can deliver him.

"Greater Sin! Greater Salvation!"
The Hour of Decision, 1961

God has not promised to deliver us from trouble; but he has promised to go with us through the trouble.

"Be Prepared"
The Hour of Decision, 1957

Billy Graham speaks of man's deep-rooted spiritual need for God, and the results of his being deprived of the fulfillment of that need:

A hungry man is a dangerous man, and a man away from God can be expected to be plagued by phobias, fears, and complexes. Why do people commit unthinkable crimes? Why do we have shocking episodes showing the bestiality of man? For the simple reason that men who have not had their basic need met—the need of being reconciled to God—are unpredictable, untrustworthy, worried, anxious creatures. Of course, most people by sheer will power are able to restrain themselves from gross crimes, but underneath the cloak of respectability seethes and surges a sinful nature that is capable of the worst evil imaginable. The very restraint exercised by modern man is one of the causes of his tension and anxieties.

"The Cure for Anxiety"
The Hour of Decision, 1957

This is the picture of modern man. He is impotent in that he knows a moral code but has no power to live up to it. He is blind to his own moral wretchedness and to his imminent destruction. Modern man is also halt and crippled. . . . Modern man has withered souls and paralyzed wills.

Madison Square Garden
New York City
May 20, 1957

This parable would be humorous if it weren't so painfully accurate:

I can take a pig, clean him up, give him a bath, put a ribbon around his neck, put a little Chanel No. 5 on him, put him in my living room, and say, "My, what a wonderful pig. He's turned over a new leaf. He has made a change."

You open the door and where does the pig go? Back to the mud. His nature has never been changed.

You get a man in church on Sunday morning, get him all dressed up, and he walks in and he looks like a saint for about an hour, looks wonderful. The collection plate comes by and he puts in a big wad.

He sits there thinking about *Gunsmoke* the night before or thinking about the golf game that afternoon, and he looks at the preacher, and the preacher thinks what he is saying is getting through.

Then he passes by the minister at the door and says, "Oh, I got a kick out of that sermon this morning," and he goes home, gets off his Sunday clothes, takes his wings off, and horns begin to grow.

All week long he is out to get the next guy, filled with jealousy, deception, and all the rest of it.

You see, his nature has never been changed. He is just like the pig.

He can dress up for an hour on Sunday and look like a saint, but the rest of the week he lives like a pig—the way he treats his wife, the money he spends on drink, the money he spends on gambling and all the other things. He needs his nature changed, and that's why Jesus said. "Ye must be born again."

"Must Be Reborn to Enter Heaven"
Houston Crusade, 1965

Most thoughtful people recognize that man is a paradox. He is both dust of earth and breath of God. He is a contradiction of discord and harmony, hatred and love, pride and humility, tolerance and intolerance, and peace and turmoil. The depths to which he sinks only dramatize the heights to which by God's grace he is capable of rising. His very misery is an indication of his potential greatness. His deep yearnings are an echo of what he might be.

"Past, Present, and Future"
The Hour of Decision, 1958

After putting mankind in its proper perspective, Billy Graham illustrates the folly and presumption of pride:

We live like a little ant on this little speck of dust out in space. We get a Ph.D. degree and we strut across the stage and say, "Well, I don't know whether there is a God or not." And we can't even control ourselves.

We can't even keep from blowing ourselves apart. We can't even keep from manufacturing nuclear weapons that could destroy the world. We can't even keep from hating each other and fighting each other and killing each other.

We can't even keep from stealing from each other. We can't even keep from dying, because all of us are going to die. We can't even keep off death and yet we claim, "Well, we can't take God, we can't believe in God."

No wonder the Bible says, "The fool hath said in his heart, there is no God," because a man that would deny the existence of God is a fool.

Eighth Sermon
Charlotte Crusade, 1958

This moving little parable beautifully illuminates the nature of Christ:

One day I was walking along the road with my little boy, who was then five years of age, and we stepped on an ant hill.

We killed a lot ants and wounded a lot of others, and I

said to Ned, "Wouldn't it be wonderful if we could go down there and help those ants rebuild their house and bury their dead, take care of their wounded?"

He said, "But, Daddy, we are too big. We can't get down there and help those ants."

I thought for a moment. "Wouldn't it be wonderful if we could become an ant and live in an ant world?"

And that is what God did. God Almighty decided to become a man and that is who Jesus Christ was.

"Why God Allows Suffering and War"
Houston Crusade, 1965

Our notions of Christ have become watered down, says Billy Graham. We have failed to remember that He was a vigorously active man as well as a spiritual being:

We have limited Christ to the sanctuary, to the temple, to the religious area of our lives. We have not practiced applied Christianity. We have restricted it to a Sunday affair. We worship Him behind thick church walls. We tuck Him away in quiet little recesses. From Sunday to Sunday He is rarely mentioned. We spend very little time reading His Word or praying. We Christians act and live as though Christ were dead.

This kind of Christ will never make an impact on the revolutionary world in which we live. This is not the Christ of the Bible. He is too weak and small; He is irrelevant. The weak, emaciated, impotent Christ of the Church of today bears little resemblance to the Christ who is found in the early Church, which dared to challenge the world and turn it upside down.

"The Risen Christ"
The Hour of Decision, 1964

I believe that Jesus Christ was the most perfectly developed physical specimen in the history of the world. He never had sin to deform his body. His mind was perfect. His nervous system was perfectly coordinated with the rest of his body.

He would have been one of the greatest athletes of all times. Every inch a man.

Third Sermon
Charlotte Crusade, 1958

In every phase of life we face this recurring question: "What think ye of Christ?" In youth, too happy to think—I've plenty of time. In manhood, too busy to think—I must make a living. In maturity, too anxious to think—I've more urgent problems. Declining years, too old to think—my pattern of life is set. As death approaches, too ill to think—my sensibilities are dulled and my mind weary. Death, too late to think—the spirit is flown, the day of opportunity is past, the harvest is gone, and now God's Judgment Day.

"Youth Aflame"
The Hour of Decision, 1959

I was invited to have coffee one morning with Konrad Adenauer before he retired as the chancellor of Germany. When I walked in, I expected to meet a tall, stiff, formal man who might be embarrassed if I brought up the subject of religion. After the greeting, the chancellor suddenly turned to me and said, "Mr. Graham, what is the most important thing in the world?"

Before I could answer, he had answered his own question. He said, "The resurrection of Jesus Christ. If Jesus Christ is in the grave, then I don't see the slightest glimmer of hope on the horizon."

Then he amazed me by saying that he believed that the resurrection of Christ was one of the best-attested facts of history. He said, "When I leave office I intend to spend the rest of my life gathering scientific proof of the resurrection of Jesus Christ."

"The Risen Christ"
The Hour of Decision, 1964

The Second Coming of Christ, prophesied in the Bible but frequently the subject of much debate, is another subject about which Billy Graham holds no doubts:

Over three hundred times the New Testament expresses the fact that Christ is going to come. This has been the hope of the Church down through the ages.

It has been called the "blessed hope," the glorious hope that Christ some day will come back to this earth again.

Ladies and gentlemen, on the dark horizon of the present moment I see no other hope. There is really no other possibility I see at the moment for solving the problems of the world than the coming again of Jesus Christ.

The world is in darkness and the darkness is growing blacker—frustration, confusion, the world on the horns of a dilemma.

Nineteenth Sermon
Charlotte Crusade, 1958

Newton had his dynamics of matter and motion. Einstein had his dynamics of relativity. But Jesus Christ has His dynamics of the Spirit. In chemistry, under given conditions, hydrogen and oxygen combine to form water. So repentance and faith in Christ produce a new life.

"Christian Conversion"
The Hour of Decision, 1959

Nature is rife with wonderful examples of new birth—all mysterious and yet wonderful. Take the lowly caterpillar. His lot seems an empty and useless one, threatened by man, beast, and fowl. But one day he climbs up into a bush and nature throws a fiber robe around him. He goes to sleep. In a few short weeks there is movement within the fibrous coat, and out of that cocoon emerges a beautiful, resplendent winged creature. He soars over the old pitfalls that used to entrap him, and like a winged angel flies from one fragrant flower to another. A natural metamorphosis? Yes! One which is not easily explained but generally accepted.

The world of nature is filled with beautiful analogies of the spiritual birth. They all speak eloquently to man, who by nature is given to evil, telling him that there is a higher, more triumphant manner of life for him. The Bible says, "Thou madest him a little lower than the angels; thou crownedst him with glory and honor" (Hebrews 2:7).

"The New Birth"
The Hour of Decision, 1955

Although man's nature is inherently sinful, his outlook is not entirely bleak; the recognition of his own deficiencies is the first step toward salvation:

When you confess with Isaiah, "I am a man of unclean lips" (Isaiah 6:5), you will stand on the threshold of a victorious life. When you face the fact of your own inadequacy, your own failure, your own sinfulness, you have taken the first step toward gaining a glorious and wonderful personal victory that will carry you through the days of crisis that lie ahead.

"Three Keys to Usefulness"
Hour of Decision, 1962

Only as we bow in contrition, confession, and repentence at the foot of the Cross, can we find forgiveness. There is the grace of God! We don't deserve it! A man said sometime ago, "When I get to the judgment of God, all that I will ask for is justice." My beloved friend, if you get justice, then you will go to hell. You don't want justice. What you want is mercy.

"The Grace of God"
The Hour of Decision, 1957

A man got up the other day at a university where I was speaking in a discussion group, and he said, "Mr. Graham, I don't believe in religion."

I said, "I agree with you. I don't believe in religion either."

He said, "What? I thought you were a religious leader."

I said, "Oh, no, you have got me wrong. I don't believe in religion, but I can tell you about a wonderful person called Jesus."

He said, "Oh."

Everybody's got religion, all over Africa. They have religion, all over India. They have religion, all over China. They have religion, all over the world—everybody has religion. Atheism may be your religion, but it is a religion. We are not calling people to religion. We are calling them to Christ, who can change your life.

"The Wickedest Man Who Ever Lived"
Houston Crusade, 1965

The nature of the Christian religion and the role of the Christian person in society are two topics frequently discussed in the sermons of Billy Graham:

What does it mean to be a Christian? Is it a person who is born in a Christian home?

No, I could be born in a garage, but that does not make me an automobile. You can be born in a Christian home and have fine Christian parents, but it does not make you a Christian. You cannot inherit Christianity.

You say, "Well, Billy, a person who lives by the golden rule, isn't that a Christian?"

Not necessarily. A Christian is a person in whom Christ dwells.

Twenty-fifth Sermon
Charlotte Crusade, 1958

And the Bible indicates that the Christian life is a life of conflict and warfare. There are some people who promise that faith in God will remove all troubles and difficulties. In fact, sometimes I think the truly committed Christian is in conflict with the society around him more than any other person. Society is going in one direction, and he is going the opposite direction. This brings about friction and conflict. But God has promised, in the midst of trouble and conflict, a genuine peace, a sense of assurance and security that the worldly person never knows.

"The Cure for Anxiety"
The Hour of Decision, 1957

Billy Graham warns against mistaking external forms for genuine religious faith and action:

You may be able to pronounce all the shibboleths. You may be able to pronounce all the clichés. You may be an orthodox of the orthodox's. You may be able to split all the theological hairs. You may be a theological bloodhound, but I tell you tonight, unless we are separated from the temper and the lusts and the evils of this world, we cannot call ourselves God's children.

Fourth Sermon
Charlotte Crusade, 1958

Although outward signs are not enough, Billy Graham believes that outward appearances are important as manifestations of the real inner qualities of the Christian:

I think that a Christian ought to look like a Christian. I've seen so many Christians slouch around. That's not God's way.

A Christian young person ought to have his shoulders up. He ought to have a clear eye. When he shakes hands with you, he ought to look you right in the eye and grip your hand.

He looks like a Christian, and he acts like a Christian.

None of this sissy, effeminate sort of business we've got now, with these long sideburns and all the rest.

Ninth Sermon
Charlotte Crusade, 1958

Billy Graham cautions his listeners against a kind of "religious relativism":

We must get away from the nonsense advocated by so many today that it doesn't matter what you believe, that we are all going to the same place, and that one religion is as good as another. It matters a great deal what you believe! We are not all going to the same place. If we are, then we might as well scrap the New Testament and turn the clock of history back to the Dark Ages.

"The Gospel for the Whole World"
The Hour of Decision, 1959

Billy Graham explains that true Christianity requires not merely consent, but also commitment:

There are three little men that live down inside of every one of us. One is intellect, another is emotion, and the third is will. Intellectually, you may accept Christ. Emotionally, you may feel that you can love Him. However, until you have surrendered to Christ by a definite act of your will, you are not a Christian.

"The Assurance of Salvation"
The Hour of Decision, 1958

The Christian life, observes Billy Graham, is not just a way of being, but also a way of acting:

There was a girl who heard one of Beethoven's sonatas. She had a strong desire to learn to play. She had real latent musical talent, but she didn't practice her piano. She never struggled with the five-finger exercises and scales, and years later her neighbors had to listen to her murder Beethoven.

Now, she wanted to play Beethoven, she wanted to be a musician, but she was not willing to practice.

Now just to *want* to live the Christian life is not enough.

You must learn *how* to live the Christian life. Attention must be given to the methods, the techniques, and the practice.

Twenty-fifth Sermon
Charlotte Crusade, 1958

Billy Graham points out, ironically, that "enthusiasm," which is derived from the Greek word for "inspired by the gods," is today tolerated in every field except religion:

Generally speaking, the world dislikes to face reality and most certainly dislikes change. It wants to know that it is comfortable and that everything is settled and established. New vices can be very disturbing. Men and women of vision and enthusiasm disturb the complacent, the smug, and the apathetic. And so the people who have their heads in the sand like the proverbial ostrich throw up their hands in horror and pass judgment on the enthusiastic ones. They call them mad; they call them beside themselves.

It is very strange that the world accepts enthusiasm in every realm but the spiritual. The world appreciates and understands emotion and enthusiasm until it becomes religious fervor—then immediately it is suspect. You can be as mad as you like about the World Series; you can go to the Yankee Stadium and shout yourself hoarse, and everyone thinks this is normal. You can be as mad as you like about money or pleasure or even drink. You can be mad about the Beatles. And in each case you are thought to be sane and normal. But bring the same enthusiasm into your moral convictions, and you are told that you are beside yourself. When you bring a grand and glorious abandon to your dedication to the Lord Jesus Christ, you are thought by many of your neighbors to be mad, to have "gone too far" in religion.

One of the great needs in the Church today is for every Christian to become enthusiastic. Shout his faith in Jesus Christ. This is the very essence of vital spiritual experience. The apostles had been with Christ, and they could not help but testify to that which they had seen and heard (Acts 4:20). Every Christian should become an ambassador of Christ with the splendid madness and gay abandon of Francis of Assisi. Every Christian should be so intoxicated with Christ and so filled with holy fervor that nothing could even quench his ardor.

However, let me warn you that when you take this position with Christ, you will be called mad, you might be persecuted—you might even be crucified. You will be accused of being beside yourself, you will be called a religious fanatic, and some will label you an extremist.

"Extremism"
The Hour of Decision, 1965

A recurring thought in Billy Graham's preachings is that today's concept of religion—a meek, passive, stagnant concept—underlies the failure of spirituality to find wide acceptance among the young:

And, then, we look at the world today and we find that young people are changing the world. You go to any part of the world today; it's the young people that are marching. Marching under various flags. Castro got the young people of Cuba, and changed Cuba. Ben Bella got the young people of Algeria to march to him. And all over the world today young people are marching. They want a song to sing, a flag to follow, a cause to believe in—something tough and hard and rugged.

Dr. Sam Procter was in my home as a guest about a month ago. He is the associate director of the Peace Corps, and he said, "You know, we found a strange and interesting and unique thing when we talked to young people about going to the Peace Corps." He said, "The rougher and the harder and the tougher we made it, the greater the response."

Young people wanted a challenge; young people wanted something that was hard and tough, and they'll respond to it. I'll tell you the gospel of Jesus Christ is hard and tough and rough. It's hard to be a Christian. It's hard to live a Christian life in this present age in which we live!

"God's Delinquent"
Recorded Sermon
Great Sermons Series

Billy Graham employs a striking metaphor to illustrate the role of the faithful in society:

The Gulf Stream is in the ocean, and yet it is not a part of it. Believers are in the world, and yet they must not be absorbed by it. The Gulf Stream maintains its warm temperatures even in the icy water of the North Atlantic. If Christians are to fulfill their purposes in the world they must not be chilled by the indifferent, godless society in which they live.

"Nonconformity to the World"
The Hour of Decision, 1953

Billy Graham can almost always be seen preaching with a copy of the Bible in his hands. Here he illustrates his views on the Holy Scriptures:

The Bible is the constitution of Christianity. Just as the United States Constitution is not of any private interpretation, neither is the Bible of any private interpretation.

Just as the Constitution includes all who live under its stated domain, without exception, so the Bible includes all who live under its stated domain, without exception. As the Constitution is absolute, so the Bible is absolute. As the Constitution is the highest law of man, so the Bible is the highest law of God. God's laws for the spiritual world are found in the Bible. Whatever else there may be that tells us of God, it is more clearly told in the Bible.

"Our Bible"
The Hour of Decision, 1957

Where the Bible is concerned, Billy Graham is uncompromising in his adherence to doctrine:

In my early teens I listened frequently to sermons on this subject [of Hell]. Once I heard a prominent preacher say that after several thousand years of suffering the wicked world will have a second opportunity for salvation. This sounded good to me. I could live as I liked here, and if I rejected salvation I would still have another chance! But as I study the word of God carefully, I do not find one verse of Scripture that even hints or indicates that there will be a second chance after death. God's Word strongly declares, "Now is the accepted time; behold, now is the day of salvation." The Bible indicates that the moment your heart stops ticking and your last breath has gone, your last opportunity of salvation has gone also.

"Hell"
The Hour of Decision, 1963

The greatest way to get through to young people is to teach them the real teachings of Christianity. I think that we [should take] the Bible in our hands and preach the Bible. This is what the Bible says, not what I say as a clergyman, but what the Bible says. And I think that young people, even today, look upon the Bible with a tremendous respect, and they want to know what it teaches, but I think there is a vast ignorance as to what it teaches.

Today
NBC Television
April 19, 1966

As in this excerpt, Billy Graham often speaks of the nature and the efficacy of prayer:

Man prays by instinct. If he has no god, he makes one. The most godless person will cry out to God in time of peril. When Mr. Khrushchev, who says he doesn't believe in God, came to London, he exclaimed one day, "My God."

That was a form of prayer, no matter how crude it was. In a moment he forgot himself and called on God.

Man prays by instinct.

Twenty-sixth Sermon
Charlotte Crusade, 1958

Billy Graham discusses the living torment of those doomed to addiction to various forms of sin:

The Bible indicates that there are three kinds of death: physical, spiritual, and eternal. All three of these deaths occur because of sin. "The wages of sin, is death." It is the eternal death that we are concerned with, the death which the Bible calls Hell.

We can see Hell's earthly counterpart all about us—suffering caused by the misuse of God's blessings. The sun is healing, but if you ignore its power you will suffer from excruciating sunburn. Water can be a boon and blessing to mankind, but if one ignores its dangers and uses it wrongly, it can drown and kill. Medicines can bring healing, but if they are misused they can bring death. Certain narcotics are a blessing to suffering humanity, but if they are misused they can bring addiction and intense misery. The law of gravity is a blessing to humanity in a thousand ways, but if it is defied it can bring death.

We can also recognize Hell's earthly counterpart in other ways. Many people live in a hell of appetite. It is estimated that we have sixty thousand dope addicts in America. Statistics show that most of them will never be cured. Ask the narcotic addict if there is a hell.

Some are living in a hell of lust and immorality. Others are living in an inforno of greed and covetousness. Still others live in hells of resentment, prejudice, intolerance, and bigotry. We fashion our earthly hells out of the passions, the selfishness, and the sin that floods into our lives. There is always plenty of material for the fabrication of a hell on earth, and many of us have made one from which we cannot extricate ourselves.

However, the Bible indicates not only that there can be

a hell of our own making on earth, but that there is a Hell in the future, toward which every man who is deliberately rejecting Christ is going.

. . .

Hell, according to Billy Graham, is a reality, whether or not we visualize it in terms of "fire and brimstone":

Whether there is really literal fire in Hell or not, all these are descriptions of God's hatred for sin and they portray a Bible truth.

Certainly Hell is not less real, but more so. Hell will be a place where the flames of lust and passion and hatred will burn throughout eternity. It will be a place where the darkness of man's sin will be unrelieved by the brightness of His presence.

If there is no fire in Hell, then God is using symbolical language to indicate something far worse. Certainly no words in any language of the world can describe the awfulness and the horribleness of spending age after age without God, without hope, without light, where the fire is never quenched and the warm dieth not.

"Hell"
The Hour of Decision, 1963

CHAPTER II:

THE HOME

The broken home has long been acknowledged as one of the primary causes of degeneracy among modern youth. Billy Graham says:

A home is like the solar system. The center, the great sun, holds the solar system together. If it were not for the sun the solar system would fly to pieces. Unless the Son of God is put at the center of your home, it, too, may fly to pieces.

. . .

Wherever the cancer of the broken home remains unchecked, this malignant growth eats its way into the vitals of national existence. This is one lesson that stands out with prominence on the pages of world history.

Almost every historian will agree that the disintegration of the Roman Empire was due largely to the broken home. In a recent study of moral conditions in Greece, Persia, and Babylonia, the scholars agreed that divorces and broken homes, more than any other single factor, contributed to the downfall of these nations.

"The Answer to Broken Homes"
The Hour of Decision, 1955

What is happening in America? Where is our sense of moral values? Have we as a people sunk so low that the only persons we are interested in reading about and seeing are the harlots and the adulterers? No wonder the American home is crumbling.

. . . Thoughtful spokesmen the world over agree that if society's health in the world is to be maintained, the home must be preserved. Only the *Communist Manifesto* disagrees. It says, "The claptrap about the family will vanish with the vanishing of Capitalism." Though none of us are in accord with this concept, yet we are yielding to pressures which are rolling away our home life.

When will we learn that houses are not homes, money is not security, gadgets cannot bring happiness, and that there are no substitutes in our home life for faith, hope, and love?

"The Home"
The Hour of Decision, 1958

Billy Graham points out that broken homes are a social problem of greater magnitude, and of greater implications, than is generally realized:

The broken home has become the Number One social problem of America, and could ultimately lead to the destruction of our civilization. Since the basic unit of any society is the home, when the home begins to break, the society is on the way to disintegration. Just as Communism, it is a threat to the American way of life. It does not make screaming headlines, but like termites, it is eating away at the heart and core of the American structure.

"The Answer to Broken Homes"
The Hour of Decision, 1955

Billy Graham deals with love and marriage:

Love—I would say physical attraction is the least of it all—is based on congeniality, getting along with each other, liking the same things, doing the same things, and spirituality.

• • •

Good advice such as the following often appears obvious, and might seem superfluous if it weren't for the fact that it is so obviously and flagrantly ignored:

Well, I've got a certain suggestion for you. . . . Before you get married, learn everything you can about the one you contemplate marrying. You know, so many people marry and they have so little knowledge of the other person; his family, his background, his habits, and all the rest.

A lot of them marry so quickly. I read about one the other day. They met in the morning, and they were married by evening. In this vitamin-capsule age in which we're living, jet-propelled marriage. And they were divorced two days later.

. . .

And I want to tell you this, I would strongly advise that if she is of another religion, that you not marry her or him because about eight out of every ten marriages are desperately unhappy. Some succeed, but most of them are unhappy.

"Youth's Problems"
Dallas, Texas
June 20, 1953

If you want trouble, if you want hell in your home, marry a person with deep-seated religious differences, and you've got it, brother.

Youth Night Service
Pittsburgh Crusade
September 12, 1952

Billy Graham indicates that we have been looking in the wrong places for the advice and understanding of marital difficulties:

It is high time that our so-called experts on marriage, the family, and the home turn to the Bible. We have read newspaper columns and listened to counselors on the radio, psychiatrists have had a land-office business. In it all, the One who performed the first marriage in the Garden of Eden and instituted the union between man and wife has been left out.

"The Answer to Broken Homes"
The Hour of Decision, 1955

Billy Graham deals sternly yet fairly with one of the greatest of responsibilities of the home:

A man who is unfaithful to his wife in thought, word, or deed has committed one of the greatest crimes known to God and man. It is one of the few sins for which God demanded the death penalty in the Old Testament. God says that no adulterer will be found in the Kingdom of Heaven. The wrath of God is waiting at the Judgment Day for any man who is unfaithful to his wife and guilty of this terrible sin. If you have committed this sin, renounce it, and then confess it to God; the Bible says, "If we confess our sins, He is faithful and just to forgive us our sins" (1 John 1:9). Yes, it is possible for you to be forgiven and cleansed at this moment.

"The Responsibilities of the Home"
The Hour of Decision, 1955

The sin of immorality is so terrible in the sight of God that it is the only thing that he allows to break the marriage relationship.

"The Answer to Broken Homes"
The Hour of Decision, 1955

But faithfulness is not the only important responsibility of the husband and father in the home:

. . . In these modern days the word father in some areas has come to mean a character with a highball in one hand, a cigarette in the other, and nothing but sinful mischief in his heart. Thank God, this is true only in a small segment of our society; but unfortunately this idea is growing as fathers take less and less responsibility in the home.

"Father"
The Hour of Decision, 1957

That Billy Graham is a man with practical experience as a husband and a father should be obvious from the following advice:

The husband should remain a lover. How long has it been since you took your wife some flowers and it wasn't an anniversary and it wasn't her birthday? You don't need to sink so far in the seat. How long has it been since you greeted her with a kiss? I'm not talking about a little peck on the cheek. I mean a kiss.

You know, it's the little things that mean a lot to the woman. It's not just the big things. It's not just buying her a Christmas present. It's every day—the thoughtful little things. If you go away, write her a card or a letter each day. It's the little things. It's the little courteous things.

The Bible says husbands ought to love their wives. Show your love to her. Help her to stay young. Hers is the hardest job of all.

Don't be a roughneck. Be a gentleman to her. Before you were married, if you came to a mud puddle, you'd take off your coat and put it down and say, "Walk on it."

Now if you come to a mud puddle, you say, "Jump, lady, I think you can make it."

And another thing, do you ever open the door of the car for her, or do you get out and tell her to get out the best she can? Of course she can get out, but it's that little extra courtesy that'll mean everything to her.

And don't be a tightwad. I don't think there's anything lower than a man that keeps all the money to himself and never gives his wife money to spend, and listen, she wants some money every week and every month which she can call her own and it's none of your business where she spends it, even if it's only fifty cents.

That's right. She may want to buy something she didn't want to tell you about. It may be a birthday present for you. She should have money because you are partners.

In God's sight, the man and the woman are partners and everything you have is half hers. In God's sight, in the sight of the courts, morally, spiritually, every way, half is hers, and she deserves to spend it like you do, a little bit for herself.

A husband is to be a real comrade to his wife. A husband is to be courteous to his wife. Husbands are to forgive their wives.

Twentieth Sermon
Charlotte Crusade, 1958

Billy Graham has more than his own experience to base his judgments on:

In one sense, the husband and wife are co-equal in the home, but when it comes to the governmental arrangement of the family, the Bible, from Genesis to Revelations, teaches that man is to be the head of the home. We have many women today in America who are wearing the trousers in the family. Some of them have to, bless their hearts, because they have married the type of man who refuses to take his proper responsibility in the home. But the principle the Bible teaches is that the husband be the head of the house.

"The Responsibilities of the Home"
The Hour of Decision, 1955

The Bible says, "Love your wife."

Now, you ought to say it sometimes with flowers, or candy, now, maybe not candy because wives are a little sensitive about that, but flowers. How long has it been since you sent your wife some flowers and it wasn't an anniversary, it wasn't her birthday, it wasn't Christmas, it wasn't Thanksgiving. You just brought her some flowers and said, "Honey, I love you."

Now, the first time you do that she may faint. You had better have a doctor present, but sometimes husbands forget that it is the little things that mean so much to the woman—that telephone call in the middle of the day when she is working hard at home and you're at the office or the factory, just slip away at the coffee break, give her a ring and say, "Honey, I love you." It would mean everything to her.

"Problems of the American Home"
Houston Crusade, 1965

The Scriptures are again the source of Billy Graham's advice to wives:

The Bible also teaches that the wife is to make the home as happy as possible. It should be a man's heaven, where he can find protection from the storms of life. It should be a safe retreat into which the problems that assail him in the outside find no entrance. His home should be a place of love and understanding. He is the king of the household, and you, his wife, are the queen. It is your duty to make the home as near like heaven as possible. There are hundreds of ways in which you can do so. You can keep the house clean and in order, you can prepare his favorite dishes and have the meals on time. You can make the home attractive and comfortable—all these things play their part.

Consider, too, that any slovenliness or carelessness in your dress or personal appearance and cleanliness will naturally lessen the admiration and love your husband has for you. You dress up for a guest—why not do the same for your husband? And don't be a lazy wife—be industrious. Then, as the Scriptures says, your husband, as well as your children, will rise up to call you blessed (Proverbs 31:28).

"The Responsibilities of the Home"
The Hour of Decision, 1955

Wives, you are to submit yourselves to your husbands. Now, I've got some suggestions for you. When he comes home from a hard day's work and you're in the kitchen, don't yell at him from the kitchen and say, "Is that you, John? Shut the door."

No, what you ought to do is dress up a little bit in the evening—fresh dress—and come and greet him with a big kiss and welcome him home. Make him feel like he's wanted. That he's somebody.

Why, he may faint the first time you do it, but try and see if it doesn't happen. And be attractive. No wonder some husbands don't want to come home.

Twentieth Sermon
Charlotte Crusade, 1958

Billy Graham points out a common denominator in the failings of today's women:

Too many women have too much leisure time for their own good. They have time for criticism, gossip, faultfinding, and complaining. They have time for idle games and far too much attention to things of the flesh. There are other women who have too little time for the enduring things of life. They are too busy flitting about doing this and that. They have great activity and much doing, but they lack time for building Christian characters. Both kinds of women—the too-idle and the too-busy—need to take time for meditation and quiet repose in prayer to

God. They need time to cultivate their souls that in turn they may cultivate the souls of their children.

"Mother's Day Message"
The Hour of Decision, 1957

Billy Graham makes these observations on the status of the woman in Christian societies:

Did you know that I have never understood how any woman could reject Christ? You're a woman here today. You are today what you are because of Christ.

I have traveled on every continent in the world. I want to tell you, in every place of the world where the influence of Jesus Christ has not gone, a woman is little more than an animal.

It was Jesus who lifted the woman to her place today. And every woman owes everything she has to Jesus Christ.

Eighth Sermon
Charlotte Crusade, 1958

For Billy Graham, the role of the mother in our contemporary society is a crucial one, for it is through the mother that Christianity can mold our children in the formative years:

Today, as the divorce rate continues to climb and the newspapers are filled with stories of violent and vicious women who spend more time in the bars than they do at home, our nation is in desperate need of consecrated Christian mothers. We need Christian mothers more than we need atomic bombs and new planes.

. . .

Emerson said, "Men are what their mothers make them." But since the world is what men make it, and men are what their mothers make them, it naturally follows that the world can be no better than its mothers.

There can be no great men without great mothers.

. . .

Some of the greatest criminals of history have had bad mothers. Most of the noble characters and fine leaders of history have had good, God-fearing mothers.

We are told that George Washington's mother was pious, and that Sir Walter Scott's mother was a lover of poetry and music. On the other hand, we are told that Nero's mother was a murderess and that the drunkard Lord Byron's mother was a proud and violent woman.

"Mother's Day Message"
The Hour of Decision, 1957

The proper upbringing of children is among the most important functions of the Christian home, and Billy Graham's advice on this subject is emphatic:

And listen to this, parents! Children are great mimics. They will not listen to you if you're living the wrong type of life or an inconsistent life. If Dad talks about constructive activity, but then he sits in front of the T.V. all evening sipping beer, his actions speak louder than his words, and the children note what he does but they forget his lectures. You teach your children not to lie, but they hear you tell little white lies over the telephone. Train a child in the way he should go, teach them the proper set of values.

What's important in your life? Is it a new television set, a new automobile—are these the things that young people look at and say, "Well, this was important in Dad's life, this was important in Mother's life. They thought more about a cocktail party than they did the church. They thought more about an automobile than they did in giving to missionaries"? What kind of values are you teaching your young people? After a while they say to heck with it all, and they rebel against you. And they rebel against your religion because they've seen the inconsistency, the hypocrisy in your life.

"God's Delinquent"
Recorded Sermon
Great Sermons Series

Billy Graham enumerates the most important duties of the good parent:

Take time to spend with your children. Give them ideals, moral and spiritual values; set a good example; plan family activities as a unit; discipline yourselves and your children. But most important of all, teach them to know God through regular family prayer. Bible reading and church attendance also helps.

New York Crusade
Summer, 1957

Parental responsibility involves giving the child what he needs, and often he needs discipline. Coddling children, sparing them from correction, is one of the primary causes of delinquency. The parent who takes the time and the trouble to discipline his child loves him far more than does the namby-pamby parent who sows the seeds of delinquency in his unspanked offspring by pampering him.

"Teen-Age Vandalism"
The Hour of Decision, 1964

We have taught our young people that morals are relative and not absolute. Kinsey has encouraged premarital experiences and our newsstands are filled with obscene literature.

Do not blame the teen-agers! Their difficulties stem from the environment we have created for them. Most of them are ordinary young people who have been taught that thrills can be found in immorality and crime. The great majority of these young vandals do not engage in their misdemeanors for money. They do it for a thrill, or because they think it's smart, or because they think they may get their name in the paper like some movie queen.

At the heart of the trouble is the failure of parents in the home. Billy Sunday, the famous evangelist, once said, "If you want to lick the Devil, hit him over the head with a cradle."

Parents today are not interested, apparently, in defeating the Devil in the home. There seems to be little parental responsibility or discipline. Children are allowed to go wild.

Where are the parents that allow their children to roam the streets after midnight? Any parent who allows his children such leniency not only is ruining the child but sinning against God.

"The Answer to Teen-Age Delinquency"
The Hour of Decision, 1955

However, Billy Graham points out, there must be a sense of purpose in the administration of discipline:

You do your children a great injustice when you do not discipline them and when you fail to teach them to discipline themselves. Of course, in disciplinary action, whatever sort it may be, you must always leave the child knowing that you love him, that you are interested in his welfare and long for his full development.

By discipline I certainly do not mean constant scolding. I do not mean continuous nagging, lecturing, or brutal spanking. Our disciplinary action should be firm, sane, fair, consistent, and, above all, it should be given in a spirit of loving helpfulness. When the child sees that we have his best interest at heart, his response will be favorable.

Another thing, you parents ought to praise your children for the good things they do. Admiration and approval are very important elements in good discipline, and if we fail to recognize them, our children may get discouraged and say, "What's the use of being good? Daddy never notices it."

"The Home"
The Hour of Decision, 1958

Parents . . . are to set an example. The other day I was sitting beside the swimming pool of the motel where I was staying. A little boy, not more than five years old, was using some of the filthiest language I have heard. His mother said, "Son you ought not to use language like that." He pranced around and stamped his foot and said, "You go to ——" to his mother! I wish I had that boy for five minutes. He would have thought he was already there! But where did he learn it? It was not his fault; it was his parents' fault. Sometimes parents wake up to discover that they have lost control of their children because they did not take charge early enough; they did not set the proper example; they did not take time with their children; they did not give love; they did not have patience; they did not give discipline—or compliments.

We hear a lot about the need to observe the law these

days. But if children do not obey their parents, they will not grow up to obey the law.

"The Days of Youth"
The Hour of Decision, 1964

Children will invariably talk, eat, walk, think, respond, and act like their parents. Give them a target to shoot at. Give them a goal to work toward. Give them a pattern which they can see clearly, and you give them something that gold and silver cannot buy.

"The Home"
The Hour of Decision, 1958

Billy Graham discusses the most important gift a parent can give to his child:

I heard about a father who gave his boy an unusual Christmas present. He wrapped up a note in a package; the note read: "Son, during the next year I am going to give you one hour every day and two hours on Sunday." The little boy ran and put his arms around his dad and said, "Oh, Dad, that's the best Christmas present I've ever had."

Your children not only require a great deal of your time, they long and hunger for it. Perhaps they do not express it, but the hunger and longing are there just the same. Be a pal to your children, love them, spend hours with them. Cut out some of your so-called "important social engagements" and make your home the center of your social life. God will honor you and your children will grow up to call you "blessed."

"Responsibilities of Parents"
The Hour of Decision, 1955

CHAPTER III:

TEEN-AGERS AND THEIR PROBLEMS

Billy Graham points up one of the most decisive lacks in the upbringing of modern youngsters:

It is not so much a problem of what is right and what is wrong as of who decides what is right and what is wrong. No longer does the teen-ager know who his master is. Everywhere I travel I find that young people want to know: "Is there a final authority?" "Is there any objective source for this authority?" When young people are left to themselves to make their own moral choices, they flounder. They are not ready for the big decisions of life. They need authority. They are insecure without it. Something inside the young person cries out in longing for someone to tell him with authority that this is right and that is wrong.

Although many do not realize it, youth demands authority. Many parents and teachers fail to realize that youth responds to rules, regulations, and discipline. Without this, they are confused and bewildered.

. . . Today's parents have helped to create the background for their children's rebellion. Many parents imply that being popular is more important than being truthful, that being successful is more important than being honest, that being busy is more important than being together, that owning a car is more important than respecting another's property. Some parents stay so busy with activities outside the home that their children are forced to get just as busy themselves or be alone. Other parents are in a constant frenzy, organizing activities for their children so that they don't have a free moment. As a result, young people have no time to get acquainted with their parents—or with themselves.

Too much emphasis is exerted both at home and at school in trying to make adults out of subteen-agers and small children. We are told that these subteens should be prepared for adjustments to adult life. But studies indicate that they are being robbed of their childhood. From both their teachers and their parents these young people are being given a false sense of values, with the result that they become psychologically and emotionally unstable.

Throughout the behavior of parents, teachers, and teenagers alike there seems to run the theme of freedom from responsibility, which leads directly to rebellion.

"Teen-Age Vandalism"
The Hour of Decision, 1964

Young people need control and authority; and without it they are unhappy, confused, frustrated, and miserable. This is one of the psychological secrets that Hitler and Mussolini used so effectively in gaining control of the youth of Germany and Italy.

"Be Ye Separate"
The Hour of Decision, 1960

The young people of today, basically, are no worse than young people of the past, but the modern generation has been neglected. The father works all day and either spends his evenings in a bar or sitting in front of the television set with no time for the children. The mother works in order to get more money to buy more gadgets. They are overlooking their primary responsibility of just being parents and loving their children.

Press Conference
New York Crusade
Summer, 1957

Young people are rebelling, but they are tragically without a cause. Along with their generation they are searching for a creed to believe, a song to sing, a flag to follow, and a slogan to shout. If our youth could know the security, the joy, and the challenge of commitment to Christ, the nation and the world could be changed.

"Youth in Rebellion"
The Hour of Decision, 1961

Billy Graham emphasizes that the difficulties we are experiencing with our youth today are the product of our way of life:

We have about five per cent of our youth in America who are getting into trouble with the authorities every year. Ninety-five per cent of our young people are not in trouble with the authorities, and I have never understood why we don't play up the good things that our youth are doing rather than the bad things.

Yet over fifty per cent of the crimes committed in America last year were committed by teen-agers, so wc have a growing problem. They are committing murder, robbery, perversions, drinking, narcotics—all the rest.

We in America are beginning to reap what we have sown. We have told our young people for years that morals were not absolute. We have told them that morals are relative: "Do what everybody else is doing. Do as you please."

We have taken religion out of our schools, out of our teaching. What do we expect? We are now reaping it among our young people, and I do not blame the teenager.

I blame this generation of older people and the generation just past for creating an atmosphere and a world in which our teen-agers are growing up.

Thirteenth Sermon
Charlotte Crusade, 1958

Billy Graham tells his listeners how the overall environment in which America's youth have grown up has fostered in them a lack of purpose:

Do you know what nearly all the sociologists say today in their study of young people? The greatest problem facing young people today is not sex, it is boredom, boredom. Did you know that when they had the riot at Hampton Beach in New Hampshire they asked the young people what was wrong, why did they do it? Many of them said, "Just for the hell of it." Bored—life has no purpose, life has no meaning. Give your life to Christ and you will never spend another bored minute.

"Youth of Today Searching for Security"
Houston Crusade, 1965

There are thousands of teen-agers rebelling against law and order. Why? Because many of them are being taught that the policeman is his enemy instead of his friend. He is being taught that it is all right to lie and break the law—and even to defy the law under certain circumstances. Therefore we have lawlessness and rebellion throughout our teen-age culture today, and it is going to be frightening in the next generation unless we can do something about it now.

Youth today is full of energy; and if that energy is not used in constructive ways, it will be used in harmful and dangerous ways. Being a dedicated Christian takes these sources of youthful energy and converts them to useful, constructive purposes.

"Teen-Age Vandalism"
The Hour of Decision, 1964

I know many students today in high school and university are always arguing and debating religion and philosophy. And you go on campus and you see some guy on every campus and he usually has a beard. I'd like to shave a few of them.

And he has a cigarette dangling out of one side and he's got a book by Jean-Paul Sartre under the other arm. And he's called an intellectual. You know, in one of the magazines this week they have an article on a certain gentleman and they say that intellectuals don't like him. Now, who are the intellectuals? Usually the intellectuals are somebody who is sort of an extreme left-winger and he's considered an intellectual especially if he smokes a pipe and has horn-rimmed glasses and sits in an ivory tower in a university.

"Youth Rioting, Rebelling, Bored"
Houston Crusade, 1965

On campus the quickest way to security is through the crowd. Precisely where students talk about being independent and on their own, you will find them practicing the most rigid conformity in dress, in speech, in moral attitudes, and in thinking. Sometimes they follow fashion at the expense of integrity. They dread to be alone. They do not want to stand out or be different. They want to conform.

After they graduate from college, many of these young people want nothing more than a good job with a big firm and a home somewhere in suburbia. But they don't find security then either. Only Jesus Christ can give you the security that you are looking for.

"The Days of Youth"
The Hour of Decision, 1964

Billy Graham discusses some important lacks in America's educational system:

One of the great burdens on my heart at this moment is the need for Christian education. Hundreds of thousands of our young people are going to secular, humanistic, and materialistic universities. Why should we Christians not provide a Christian education in a spiritual atmosphere for these students?

So enamored are we with knowledge that about the only qualification you need in order to teach even in one of our denominational schools today is an academic degree. There is little requirement even in many of our religious schools for moral and spiritual qualifications or for theological soundness. This has led to a weakening of faith among many of our students, and subsequently a laxity and apostasy in our churches.

• • •

Billy Graham points out a failing in the modern system of education, which supplies knowledge but ignores the instruction which might give access to wisdom:

We are teaching thousands of young people in this country knowledge; but we are not helping them to know how to use that knowledge. In every area of life people are floundering, suffering from neurosis and psychological problems on a scale that we have never known before. Our heads are empty. We have educated men without indicating the source of wisdom, and we have sent them out into the world confused, bewildered, and frustrated, without moral moorings.

The Bible teaches that the prevalence of knowledge without wisdom is one of the unmistakable "signs of the end" that Jesus talked about.

"There's a Great Day Coming"
The Hour of Decision, 1961

Separation of Church and state was never meant to separate schoolchildren from God! This trend to extricate God and moral teachings from the school is a diabolical scheme, and is bearing its fruit in the deluge of juvenile delinquency that is overwhelming our nation!

"Christian Philosophy of Education"
The Hour of Decision, 1959

You know the most miserable person in the world? You know what it is? A young person outside the will of God! They're trying to hold on to the world and trying to hold on to the Lord, and they're like straddling a barbed-wire fence. They're neither fish nor fowl! And they're miserable! Get in the will of God, and you're going to be the happiest kid in town.

"Youth's Problems"
Dallas, Texas
June 20, 1953

Billy Graham voices his belief that religious involvement is the answer to modern youth's uncompromising search for meaningful commitment:

All over the world tonight young people are searching for security. They want to be controlled, they want a master, they want a center to life, they want something to believe in. I believe that Jesus Christ can become the Controller. He can become the Master. He can become the Lord of your life.

In Russia today young people are disciplined. I have a friend who has just returned from Russia, he's been there for several weeks. He said he never saw a lewd picture. He said, "I never saw a drunk person"; he said, "I went to the universities, I went to the schools and I found dedication and discipline in hard work," because, he said "the Soviet Union believes in something."

They have an ideology, they have a control, they have a security in their state in Communism.

And, ladies and gentlemen, I believe that one of the problems among teen-agers today is that they need something to believe in. They need a cause. They need a challenge. They need a flag to follow. They want a master, they want someone to control them; just as Hitler was able to get the youth of Germany, and Mussolini was able to get the youth of Italy, and the Communists were able to get the youth of Eastern Europe.

I believe that Jesus Christ can capture the youth of America. Let's march under His flag and under His banner, giving ourselves completely to Him without reservation.

I believe this will be an answer to this search for security on the part of youngsters.

Third Sermon
Charlotte Crusade, 1958

Again Billy Graham advocates a solution to the problem which identifies the fundamental causes rather than the external manifestations:

Rebellion among teen-agers can be conquered and cured if we follow a course of intelligent, sincere Christian action. It cannot be alleviated by wishful thinking or by a hand-wringing attitude or by unjustified criticism. We must recognize where the basic problem lies. It cannot be solved by the sociologists, psychologists, or law-enforcement officers alone.

The Scriptures warn us again and again that Satan himself is the leader of lawlessness and that in the end rebellion against law and order will be on the increase. Satan has control of thousands of young persons whose hearts have never been regenerated by Jesus Christ, and Satan is desperately determined to destroy America from the inside and to gain his ultimate purpose of world domination. He has hundreds of his agents writing pornographic and sadistic literature to destroy the minds of our youths. He has hundreds of others who make certain kinds of films to bring the morals of our young people a notch lower.

Satan has intellectuals in high places who write books advocating a "do-as-you-please" philosophy. For years his agents have sought to destroy the religious faith of our students. He has other agents who seek to break up the American home, which is the basic unit of our society. Any life which is not controlled by Christ can be used by Satan.

Many times the person is not aware that he is an agent of a supernatural power which is seeking to destroy the Kingdom of God—and to destroy our nation. Consciously or unconsciously the entire country is engaged at this hour in a mighty tremendous spiritual warfare. The Bible warns that there will be a time when the very elect—that means the Christians themselves—will be deceived. In other words, there will be a time when the Christian Church itself will be deceived by the clever manipulations of Satan.

"Teen-Age Vandalism"
The Hour of Decision, 1964

CHAPTER IV:

AMERICA'S DEGENERACY

We are rich in the things that perish, but poor in the things of the spirit. We are rich in gadgets, but poor in faith. We are rich in goods, but poor in grace. We are rich in know-how, but poor in character. We are rich in words, but poor in deeds. We say we are rich, but in God's estimate we are wretched, miserable, poor, blind, and naked.

"Challenge to America"
The Hour of Decision, 1963

The poorest person in this audience tonight is rich by the world's standards, and in spite of our riches, in spite of our high standard of living, our whole economy is geared to getting more.

The capitalist wants more profit. The laboring man wants more wages, for less hours. And all of us are engaged in a mad race, trampling over each other, cheating each other, lying, stealing, any way we can get it, to get another dollar.

Fourth Sermon
Charlotte Crusade, 1958

Despite all of materialism's physical advantages, it leaves one whole set of man's needs unfulfilled:

We thought if we had two chickens in every pot and two cars in every garage and a television set in every room that we would be happy. But we've found that we're not happy even when we have it all. There's something missing. There's something lacking. What is it?

Madison Square Garden
New York City
May 15, 1957

Billy Graham illustrates that the absence of God in the human heart has left room for a variety of decadent replacements:

The human heart is never a vacuum. If the heart of man is not attuned to God, it becomes a catch basin for every conceivable device of the Devil. One of the things Christ warned us against was drunkenness. Alcoholism is one of our most critical problems today. Alcoholism in the United States is now seven times more prevalent than cancer. The alarming growth of drunkenness cannot be ignored or winked at. To remove moral restraints from society is like taking the bridle off an unbroken horse.

On the newsstands across the country can be bought some of the filthiest literature I have ever seen, completely protected by recent rulings of the Supreme Court. The result is a generation which is surfeiting itself on the appetites of the flesh, to the complete dulling of its spiritual nature and the muting of the voice of conscience. Obsession with sex is evident throughout the length and breadth of the land.

One newspaper columnist commented that more space was given to the love affair of Elizabeth Taylor and Richard Burton than to the combined flights of our five astronauts who risked their lives to bring space travel into realization. Advocates of sex freedom have made a concerted effort to destroy what they term old-fashioned morals. When one considers the forced marriages, the unwed mothers, the growth of venereal disease, our crowded detention homes, and our divorce record, one would be willing to admit that they have been successful.

"Challenge to America"
The Hour of Decision, 1963

Billy Graham explains the cause of America's degeneracy:

We must face it. We've lost God. We've lost our contact with the Almighty. We've lost our anchorage; we've lost our mooring; we've lost our moral direction; we've lost our spiritual sensibilities; we've lost our contact with the supernatural, with the harmonizer and coordinator of the universe. There is a lack of a sense of life in America today.

Madison Square Garden
New York City
May 15, 1957

Billy Graham points out that one of the most insidious effects of material comfort is its destruction of the will, the strength, and the courage to act:

While the world totters on the brink of destruction, millions snore in comfortable complacency and "couldn't care less." With incomes in the United States at an all-time high, we indulge our every whim and purr contentedly like overfed cats. We have forgotten that the price of freedom is eternal vigilance!

When I was in the hospital in Hawaii, I read again of the shocking events which led up to the destruction of the United States fleet at Pearl Harbor. On that fateful day of December 7, 1941, the Japanese attacked. We know now that that attack was invited by our failure to be always vigilant. The result was the destruction of our fleet—the cause was tragic indifference.

. . . When comfort and ease and pleasure are put

ahead of duty and conviction, progress is always set back. What makes us Christians shrug our shoulders when we ought to be flexing our muscles? What makes us apathetic in a day when there are loads to lift, a world to be won, and captives to be set free? Why are so many bored when the times demand action? Christ told us that in the last days there would be an insipid attitude toward life.

"Challenge to America"
The Hour of Decision, 1963

Billy Graham's parody of the Biblical Beatitudes emphasizes the shift which has taken place in America's system of values:

The theme of our generation is: "Get more, know more, and do more" instead of "Pray more, be more, and serve more."

"Blessed are the promotors, for they get ahead in the world."

"Blessed are the intelligent, for they know their way around."

"Blessed are the clever, for they know how to get things done."

"Blessed are the research men, for they supply us with more gadgets."

"Blessed are the economists, for they bring us more prosperity."

"Blessed is the government, for it gives us security."

"Blessed are the envious, for they keep up with the Joneses."

"Blessed is our employer, for he gives us more money and better working conditions."

How different are our beatitudes from the Beatitudes of our Lord!

"The Tyranny of Time and Space"
The Hour of Decision, 1957

Billy Graham sees modern moral relativism as one of the primary agents of the decay of American values:

Modern social righteousness often differs from the righteousness of the Bible. Someone has said, "A wrong deed is right if the majority of people declare it not to be wrong." By this principle we can see our standards shifting from year to year according to the popular vote. Divorce was once frowned upon by society, and laws against fornication and adultery were strictly enforced. But now divorce is accepted by society, fornication is glorified in much of our literature and films, and perversion is looked upon as a biological abnormality rather than a sin.

"Confusing Evil with Good"
The Hour of Decision, 1964

Billy Graham categorizes several of the major political social, and scientific phenomena of modern times:

The first half of the twentieth century might well be characterized by historians as the age of delusion. This era of history marked the use of Marxism. During these fatal years free nations tried in vain to achieve peace in two World Wars. During this period nation rose against nation, and hatreds were fanned to an all-time high as international tensions added fuel to the flame. The science revolution has produced an overemphasis on the secular but a decline of faith and principle. Modern living has transformed the family and is now producing problems such as teen-age delinquency and an epidemic of divorce.

Sin is being explained away by psychological terminology. God is portrayed as a sentimental creature who never lets His wrath fall on anyone. Thousands of Americans are enamored and deluded by philosophies that are destroying the strength of the nation and threatening our security. Surely we are living in the day of which Paul warns when he says, "And with all deceivableness of unrighteousness of them that perish; because they received not the love of trust, that they might be saved and for this cause God shall send them strong delusion, that they should believe a lie; that they all might be damned who believe not the truth, but had pleasure in unrighteousness" (2 Thessalonians 2:10-12).

"Delusion or Deliverance?"
The Hour of Decision, 1961

Billy Graham denies that America's ills are social. The symptoms of the disease may be social, but the germ is man's sinfulness:

As we read the screaming headlines every day and watch the terrifying news events on television, we Americans ask ourselves, "Where have we failed?" Some people have a tendency to blame the Congress or the President. Some say that it is our misguided foreign policy. Still others contend that it is the disintegration of our family life. Others say it is a change from a rural to an urban society. Others are beginning to blame the Church, saying that the Church is guilty of neglecting the spiritual side of man. Other experts say that it is our disregard for authority. They point out that last year one of every eight police officers in America was attacked during the course of duty; 113 police officers were killed.

While all these and many others have credence, they still fall short of our real cause of failure. All these are only symptoms—the result of a deep underlying disease. What is that disease? According to the Bible, the disease is sin. We are spiritually sick. Our generation has been living like parasites on the spiritual capital of their predecessors; but we have exhausted that capital. In desperation we look this way and that, while all the time the Bible (that is lying on the shelves of almost every home and that is in almost every hotel room) has the answer to our problems—if we would only open the Bible, believe the Bible, and then do what the Bible teaches.

"It Is Time to Seek the Lord"
The Hour of Decision, 1966

Billy Graham discusses the process by which man has come to worship his own power over that of God:

During the past generation man in his incredible arrogance imagined himself entirely sufficient unto himself.

The astounding expansion of natural science and technology fostered the illusion that human welfare was simply a matter of increasing economic productivity and industrial power. Progress became the new catchword, replacing the older, now obsolete notion of salvation. In morals and philosophy in social life, even in religion, man —omnipotent man—became the master of all things. Intoxicated with his success, man denied God, because he could imagine no power superior to his own. Many men transformed themselves into gods and began worshiping themselves in their own power. During the past generation it has been an appalling idolatry, and its consequences have been two World Wars and the terrifying possibility of a hydrogen-bomb war.

One of the encouraging signs is that we are beginning to realize our sins and mistakes of the past and are gradually, as a nation, turning back to God. America, in trying to gain the world, has come very close to losing her own soul.

"Americanism"
The Hour of Decision, 1956

The fallacy of man's aspirations for perfection is that he himself is imperfect, hence incapable of creating anything perfect:

Fallible men cannot create an infallible society, but redeemed men can redeem society. You can't produce a Great Society with men who hate, connive, take advantage, pillage, and overrun, with self-interest as the motivation. National greed and selfishness are the corporate expression of self-interest, and Jesus predicted that it would still exist in the last agonizing days of man's world. . . . This self-interest must be eliminated by the transforming power of Christ if we are to be part of a Kingdom Society.

"The Kingdom Society"
The Hour of Decision, 1965

The same symptoms that were in Rome in its last days are now seen and felt in America. Walk down the streets of our cities and see the names of the films. They are either psychopathic or they are sex, many of them. What is this country coming to? I tell you we need a moral revival. We need a spiritual revival that will put a new moral fiber into our society, or we are done for before the Communists ever get here. We are being softened up right now for the kill. . . . We are being threatened today by racial tension, strife that could bring about a cold war between our great races in this country. I want to tell you this: after traveling all over the world I am convinced that one of the greatest black eyes to American prestige abroad is our racial problem in this country. It is high time that we come to the foot of the Cross. When you come to the foot of the Cross and receive Christ as Saviour, He gives you the capacity to love your neighbor. I tell you there is no superior race in God's sight. God does not look upon the outward appearance. God looks upon the heart.

"Four Great Crises"
The Hour of Decision, 1957

Billy Graham draws another unnerving parallel between the ancient Roman Empire before its collapse and modern America:

In a decadent society the will to believe, to resist, to contend, to fight, to struggle, is gone. In place of this will to resist there is the desire to conform, to drift, to follow, to yield, and to give up. This is what happened to Rome, but it also applies to us. The same conditions that prevailed in Rome prevail in our society. Before Rome fell, her standards were abandoned, the family disintegrated, divorce prevailed, immorality was rampant, and faith was at a low ebb. As Gibbon said, "There was much talk of religion, but few practiced it." Today our churches are filled, but how many are actually practicing Christianity in daily life?

"It Is Time to Seek the Lord"
The Hour of Decision, 1966

History suggested that a mass use of artificial stimulants and sedatives is indicative of a decadent civilization. Preoccupation with pleasure is a certain sign of the boredom and purposelessness within our social structure.

Young people are only resorting to an escapism that they have copied from their elders. Brought up in a society that has substituted cocktails for meditation, pleasure for prayer, and whoopee for worship, they are following the only philosophy they know: to eat, drink, and be merry, for tomorrow they may die. And the Church, tragically, is at least partially responsible for this situation.

The older generation has been too busy amassing fortunes, clipping investment coupons, reading racy novels, gazing at television, striking for higher wages, lusting after gold, keeping up with the Joneses, and playing with their gadgets. They cannot be bothered about the moral and spiritual example that they are setting for the next generation.

"Youth in Rebellion"
The Hour of Decision, 1961

Culture is a mollifying ointment rubbed on externally. It cannot reach down to man's deepest need any more than vaseline can heal cancer. Culture is desirable and commendable, but when it is cultivated to the neglect of Christ, it is like putting varnish over a scarred, marred, ugly piece of furniture—it only magnifies the defects.

The divorce rate is as high, or higher, among our so-called cultured groups as it is among the illiterate classes. And as many juvenile delinquents come from homes on the "right" side of the tracks as from the so-called "wrong" tracks. It is ironic that thousands of our prison inmates are college graduates and come from the upper bracket of our society. Culture in itself has not kept us from immorality, crime, and the eternal problem of sin; and yet many are saying . . . "Are not the rivers of culture better than the waters of God?

. . .

In our quest for the acquisition of "culture," we have concentrated on the external superficialities while ignoring the more genuine inner qualities:

Culture's virtue is its subtle danger. It stresses the importance of appearances and superficialities and tends to neglect the soul's need of inner cleansing and forgiveness.

God is not concerned with the man you seem to be—He is interested in dealing with the man you really are.

. . . Man judges by the quality of another's clothes, his Dun and Bradstreet rating, the kind of car he drives, the clubs to which he belongs, and the church which he attends. But to God these things are only a thin veneer. God looks directly upon the heart—upon its attitudes, its humility, and its pride. He makes His appraisal on the basis of what the man really is.

"The Rivers of Damascus"
The Hour of Decision, 1956

Billy Graham offers these remarks on the subject of racial discrimination, its causes and its cures:

The Athenians were proud. They thought no one was superior to them, and we have today our social snobbery, our intellectual pride, and our racial superiority.

But God says we come from the same blood. We had the same first parents. Whether your skin is dark or light, no matter what shape and size you may be, we are all the same in God's sight. We come from the same blood.

Racial tension today is increasing in the world. In some areas it is already flaming into underground warfare. Being born black in some parts of the world, Jewish in other parts, or Oriental in others, or white in some places, imposes burdens while those who are accidentally born in the ruling majority enjoy advantages they have not always earned, and for which they seem to have little appreciation.

To hate, to discriminate against those who look different, who talk different, who have different national backgrounds, or who act differently from the dominant group, is a universal trait of human nature. Racial prejudice is not limited to the southern part of the United States or Southern Rhodesia. I have observed it all over the world. Where two races live side by side, there exists prejudice.

. . . I say today there is only one possible solution and that is a vital experience with Christ on the part of both races. In Christ the middle wall of partition is broken down, the Bible says. There is no Jew or Gentile or black or white or yellow or red. We could be one great brotherhood in Christ.

However, until we come to recognize Him as The Prince of Peace and receive His love in our hearts, the racial tensions will increase.

Closing Sermon
Houston Crusade, 1965

Billy Graham points out that the problem of racial prejudice is not a particularly American problem, but rather a human one:

The race problem is not limited to any one city, nor any one part of the United States. The race problem is a world-wide problem. Wherever two races or two nationalities or even two religious groups live together, there is friction and misunderstanding.

In the last twenty years the world has become a neighborhood without being a brotherhood. The problem on

Cyprus, the problem in the Middle East between Jew and Arab, the problem in British Guiana between Indian and Negro, the problem of caste in India, and many of the deep problems that divide people all over the world are basically race problems.

For years Northern cities pointed their accusing, self-righteous fingers at the South, but now the race problem has moved to Boston, Cleveland, Chicago, New York; and we are beginning to see that under certain circumstances all of us are capable of prejudice. This also includes the Negro. Many Negroes have admitted to me that they are prejudiced and have hate in their hearts against the white man. Prejudice and hate are wrong whenever they exist.

"The Risen Christ"
The Hour of Decision, 1964

Billy Graham warns of the possible consequences of racial hatred and the violence it spawns:

This wave of bombing which is taking place in schools and synagogues and churches is symptomatic of the very things that brought Hitler to power in Germany a few years ago.

I think that every Christian should deplore it, whatever we think about the race problem. All of us are opposed to sticks of dynamite being thrown at churches and synagogues and schools, endangering lives. I am sure we are all opposed to violence; and I think that you would join me in saying tonight that we ought to pray that this spirit of restlessness and hatred and bitterness will somehow be brought to an end, because this could become very serious.

This could eventually lead to the forces of crime and the hate groups in this country taking advantage of a crisis, which could lead to anarchy and Communism.

Twenty-second Sermon
Charlotte Crusade, 1958

There are men who say they love Jesus, but hate a man because his skin is a different color. That is a sin not only against the Commandment to love thy neighbor, but it is also taking God's name in vain. It is also murder, for to hate is to wish someone dead.

Madison Square Garden
New York City
May 21, 1957

Our literature, many of our films, and our everyday lives are riddled with sexual filth. Obscenity and profanity are heard everywhere. We have fallen down before the god Aphrodite, and the Seventh Commandment has been shattered into a thousand pieces—immorality among rich and poor—perversion among the educated and the illiterate—divorce rates climbing annually—Reno overcrowded—thousands of homes collapsing because of the unfaithfulness of husband or wife or both—children running the streets as sheep having no shepherd. These are products of moral declination. And above the din can be heard the voice of God's judgment: Shall I not avenge myself on a nation such as this? Shall I not punish them for these things? For God said: I have not changed. As I allowed judgment to come to Israel long ago, I shall allow judgment to come to America unless you repent of your sins.

"God's Warning"
The Hour of Decision, 1957

I seriously doubt if the average Christian parent realizes the extent of immorality that exists among teen-agers today. It seems that the dam of morality has broken and a flood is filling the entire nation.

How can we account for this phenomenal increase in youthful immorality? Thoughtful people are more and more coming to the inescapable conclusion that the flood of lewd, obscene literature flaunted before our nation's youth—some of it under the guise of "art"—is one of the major causes of sex delinquency and crime.

"Moral Degeneration and Its Cure"
The Hour of Decision, 1959

The moral degeneracy, says Billy Graham, has proliferated into many areas of culture and entertainment:

Now new and immoral pictures are coming to America from Europe. Probably the most immoral picture ever made is one called *La Dolce Vita,* from Italy. This picture has already made twenty-eight million dollars before its arrival in America. It is a panoramic study of modern-day society in Italy. It shows Rome as dazzling with light and jumpy with jazz, constantly on the go, and forever bored. It shows Romans drowning themselves in imported Scotch and flailing wretchedly in a mass of self-content. It is so filled with sex, we are told, that it is sickening. Yet pictures of this type are now being welcomed to the United States, and millions of our teen-agers will go to see them and absorb them.

These pictures could not have been shown on our screens even five years ago. We are in the midst of a moral revolution that is going to destroy America long before Communist rockets, unless there is a complete reversal of the trend. This moral revolution that has been taking place in the last five years is changing the lives of men and women more radically than any other revolution in American history. The moral degeneration drastically affects the life of every American, deeply disturbs the community, and decisively influences the future of society. Immorality and impurity have penetrated almost every area of Western culture.

In the realm of literature there is a growing preoccupation with the subsocial sewers. Filthy pornographic and obscene books are now on the shelves of most drugstores and newsstands throughout America. Millions of old and young alike are feeding on them every week. The literature of fifty years ago has been displaced by various kinds of abnormal, perverse, vulgar, exotic, and even monstrous forms. The impure influence is also felt in the realm of music. In the bulk of night clubs and radio entertainment, music has become seductive, sensual, and perverse.

"Moral Degeneration"
The Hour of Decision, 1961

The pornography and decadence which finds its expression in many of the arts is symptomatic of a disease which is not peculiar to America:

The Western world's sole objective seems to be success, status, security, self-indulgence, pleasure, and comfort. What I am saying about America can be applied to many countries throughout the world. We can judge our times by the paintings produced by some modern artists. We see indiscriminate splashes of color with no recognizable pattern of design. The incomprehensible mixture of pigment merely denotes the confused minds and values of our day. Many of the playwrights, novelists, and script writers for television and movies give us unadulterated doses of violence, sex, and murder. Ours indeed is a sick generation in need of salvation.

"It Is Time to Seek the Lord"
The Hour of Decision, 1966

In this age of cynicism and bitterness we have become past masters at the art of profanity and obscenity. We hear filthy talk on television, in modern movies, and in private conversation. The words "damn" and "hell" are bandied about as nonchalantly as simple words like "and" and "well." Our throats have become an "open sepulcher" from which all kinds of putrefaction and filth emanate.

But profanity is not the only thing that comes out of our mouths. Irreverence, uncouthness, and rudeness, criticism, gossip, and slander proceed from the mouths of those who are under the sentence of death. Respect for

God always engenders a respect for the dignity of the individual; and when God finds no place in our lives and in our talk, disrespect for others flows out of the cesspool of our conversation. Many of our modern writers are so filled with sin that they can only think the dirty and the evil and the obscene.

"The Living Dead"
The Hour of Decision, 1964

Billy Graham deplores the effect of mass entertainment and its abuses upon the nation's peace of mind:

The main themes of radio, television, and motion pictures center largely in selfishness, materialism, revenge, greedy manipulation, and worldliness in all its phases, things with no spiritual, permanent value. They will all pass away quickly. The ideals and purposes of the Christian must reach out beyond the present moment and pierce eternity. Man's spiritual needs, his sacrifice and love for others, his willingness to look beyond rewards of the moment to find genuine happiness—these are almost foreign to the presentation of theater, radio, or television.

In addition to the anti-Christian ideals set forth in most of the entertainment world, there is a ghastly waste of time and deadening of the human mind. These media tend to destroy creative thinking; they waste our abilities to do, to create, to be—and most certainly they destroy our spiritual life.

No wonder that last year something like seventeen million Americans suffered from some form of mental or emotional disorder. Nearly two million received hospital or psychiatric clinical treatment, the bill for this care totaling over three billion dollars. Tension, frustration, complexes, and the emotional drain required to cope with a fast-moving materialistic age is rapidly destroying our peace of mind. All of these things are interrelated.

"Worldliness"
The Hour of Decision, 1960

Reliance upon mass media, claims Billy Graham, seems to be robbing Americans of their desire and ability for thought and worship:

America seems to be pleasure-mad. We have to be amused morning, noon, and night. Television is making a tremendous change in America's spiritual sensitivity. I have had pastor after pastor write me and tell me that he can see the difference in the spiritual life of his congregation since television came. People have to be amused, and we do not have time for thought, meditation, prayer, and Godly pursuits, as we used to.

One of America's greatest television comedians recently said that he does not know one happy comedian in show business. The men that make us laugh the most are the most miserable themselves.

. . . Even our comedians have a distress of soul. They are finding out that pleasure is only a veneer and does not veil the demands of the heart and soul.

"The Rivers of Damascus"
The Hour of Decision, 1956

In some of our television advertisements, we are led to believe that the greatest catastrophe that could come upon a man would be to have "five o'clock shadow," yellow teeth, or a cough in the T-zone. Undue emphasis upon the importance of the body has created a system of thought which is more concerned with the accommodations of life's journey than with its destination.

"The Time for Anxiety"
The Hour of Decision, 1957

Billy Graham describes the symptom of escapism in America's moral and spiritual decay:

A new word has entered our vocabulary, called "escapism." We Americans are trying to escape from reality. We are taking dope, drink, tranquilizing pills, entertainment, and are intent upon soul-forgetfulness.

People flee from themselves to become lost in the clouds, and the heroes of modern pictures and films are spiritually homeless. Look at the television programs. How many deal with psychological cases? Every time you look at *Gunsmoke* it sets a psychological problem dressed in Western clothes.

Opening Sermon
Charlotte Crusade, 1958

Escapism is an unconscious mechanism to escape reality. It is a mode of behavior adopted to evade unpleasant facts and realities, but it never really works.

One of our psychological problems today is group-think. We tend to act and talk like those around us, and one of our most deep-seated fears is that we might be called an outsider. This fear has led us down the road to conformity, has put the imprint of the organizational man on our souls, and robbed us of originality of thought, individual personality, and constructive action. It has invaded not only our secular life but our religious life as well, and for the vast majority of American Christians, going to church is the nice and proper thing to do on Sunday.

It advertises their respectability, gives them a warm feeling that they are behaving in a way that God-fearing ancestors would approve, and adds a few cubits to their social stature by throwing them in with a social group with whom they wish to be identified.

The group-think pressure affects our voting at the polls, the brands of food we buy at the grocery, the makes of cars we drive, the brands of gasoline we burn, as well as our patterns of religious belief.

Even from this group-think we need to be saved. We are in danger of becoming a robot civilization, manipulated by mass media, pressurized by conformity, and pushed by political maneuvers. We have developed a department-store mind where we shop for name brands of faith, politics, and a way of life. We are collectivizing the mentality of America.

Did you know that in the last election the pollsters told us to the very percentage point how we were going to vote? For the next election, I don't think we ought to have an election, just let the pollsters tell us whom we are for and it will save millions of dollars, and all that hullabaloo. Let's just put him in.

"Saved or Lost"
Houston Crusade, 1965

Closely linked with the tendency toward escapism is a notable sense of indifference toward the moral crises confronting the people:

The crack in the moral dam is widening, but like the people of Noah's day before the Flood, life goes on as usual, with only a few concerned and only a minority alarmed. However, apathy will not deter catastrophe. The people of Noah's day were not expecting judgment, but it came. We have become soft and comfortable. Watching television, I notice that when any crisis arises on the screen, the actor usually says, "Give me a drink." When the headlines get black, the sale of alcohol and barbiturates rises in the country as millions try to escape from the grim realities of our dangers.

"It Is Time to Seek the Lord"
The Hour of Decision, 1966

There is a hopelessness and a pessimism in the air not felt by any previous generation. Bars and night clubs are filled with people who are saying, "What's the use? Let's eat, drink, and be merry, for tomorrow we may die." Our revelry, our desperate pleasure-seeking, our thoughtless actions, our drunkenness, our obsession with sex, even our juvenile delinquency are all expressions of a pessimism, a despair, peculiar to this death-sentence generation.

We are like a convict condemned to death who is given his choice of food and drink before he walks the last mile. There is a sense of impending doom in the world. There is a feeling in the air that something terrible is about to happen. There is a growing conviction that things cannot go on as they are.

We are the living dead, who walk but have little goal or destination. We talk emptily about all the things that do not matter, but are silent and unconcerned about eternal values. We are like men under hypnosis: we seem to be under the spell of a power outside ourselves. We are men who have wrestled with principalities and powers, against spiritual wickedness in high places (Ephesians 6:12)—and lost.

"The Living Dead"
The Hour of Decision, 1964

Billy Graham identifies boredom as one of the most pervasive of America's spiritual ills:

Modern living, with its gadgets flowing from the production line, has created a new disease called "boredom." Even young people who should be filled with the joy of living are bored. We have machines to tone our muscles, to milk our cows, to count our money, to X-ray our bodies. We push buttons to light our homes, to wash our clothes, to start our vehicles, to beat our eggs, to mix our drinks, to bake our bread, and to provide our entertainment.

Yet with all these conveniences, man still has found no cure for boredom. Each generation becomes more addicted to the sedatives of life to dull the pain of living. Oppressed by a sense of triviality and thwarted purpose, men find no great goal or commitment to draw them, and no inner stimulation to give meaning to their existence.

"What God Can Do for You"
The Hour of Decision, 1956

Billy Graham is familiar with the works of many modern writers whose themes reflect the pessimism and despair of contemporary man:

You read Hemingway, Eugene O'Neill, Jean-Paul Sartre, Albert Camus, many of the modern writers. All of them are searching for a meaning and purpose to life and to human existence, but they can't find it. So they say, "Life is meaningless, life has no meaning."

"Why God Allows Suffering and War"
Houston Crusade, 1965

Modern writers depict the pessimism of our time and many of them throw up their hands in despair and say, "There is no answer to man's dilemma."

Hemingway once said, "I live in a vacuum that is as lonely as a radio tube when the batteries are dead and there is no current to plug into." Eugene O'Neill in *Long Day's Journey into Night* typifies the philosophical attitude of our day. He says, "Life's only meaning is death."

I say to Hemingway and O'Neill, who have already gone on, there is more to life than death. There is more to life than a radio tube that needs a place to plug into. Jesus taught us the dignity and the importance of being a person. God put us on this earth for a purpose, and our purpose is fellowship with God and to glorify God.

Closing Sermon
Houston Crusade, 1965

Billy Graham identifies the source of another one of the most widely known of America's symptoms, anxiety:

As a result of our departure from God, this has been an age of frustration; this has been an age of nervous tension. . . .

We are a nation of pill-takers. We take millions of sleeping pills every night to put us to sleep and bolster tablets in the morning to wake us up. This has been an age of selfishness, when every man has been out to get everything he could for himself, even if it meant trampling his fellow man under him.

"Americanism"
The Hour of Decision, 1956

Historians will probably call our era "the age of anxiety." Though we have less to worry about than previous generations, we have more worry. Though we have it easier than our forefathers, we have more uneasiness. Though we have less real cause for anxiety than our predecessors, we are inwardly more anxious. Callused hands were the badge of the pioneer, but a furrowed brow is the insignia of modern man.

"The Cure for Anxiety"
The Hour of Decision, 1957

. . . This has been an age of nervous tension. I think this will possibly go down in history as the "Vitamin Capsule age." The pill business is one of the best investments that you can make in America because Americans have gone crazy over pills. Big pills, little pills, square pills, round pills, oblong capsules, Dexedrine tablets to wake us up, barbiturate pills to put us to sleep at night, and a lot of aspirin thrown in in between!

"The Holy Spirit and Revival in our Time"
Convention of the National Association of Evangelicals
Chicago, 1952

When has there been a moment when the American people had such prosperity and when there are so many mental breakdowns? Psychiatry is busy today with nervous breakdowns in such a frantic effort to patch up our jangled nerves that I am told psychiatrists are going to each other for help.

Do you know how many chronic alcoholics we have in America? We have five million. Think of it! Five million chronic alcoholics in America.

You know how many sleeping pills we take every night? Twenty-one million! Twenty-one million sleeping pills a night, to put us to sleep. I don't know how many wake-up pills we use to get us up.

How many people are taking tablets and pills just to dull them from the realities of life?

Never before in history has there been a nation that had so much and is so bored with life.

Fourteenth Sermon
Charlotte Crusade, 1958

Psychiatric treatment, a relatively new therapy, can relieve the mind; physicians can help the body; but only God can save the soul. The basic cause of much of our anxiety is beyond the reach of the psychiatrist and the physician. They tinker with the symptoms of anxiety, but only God has the cure.

. . .

Now, the genius of modern psychiatry is that it probes into the minds of men for the cause of their phobias and frustrations. But the genius of the gospel of Christ is that it has diagnosed the soul of man, revealed his need, and provided a cure.

"The Cure for Anxiety"
The Hour of Decision, 1957

Billy Graham outlines three of the gravest dangers confronting America and threatening her existence:

As I see it, America is facing a number of enemies. But there are three primary enemies that I would like to mention at this moment.

First, there is moral deterioration. A moral breakdown of frightening proportions threatens to engulf the nation. Unless the moral structure and political integrity of the nation are rebuilt, the nation cannot survive. A great spiritual awakening is invariably God's remedy for moral degeneration.

The second enemy that America faces is inflation caused by greed and selfishness. If we go on spending ourselves deeper in debt, it will only be a matter of time until the American dollar will lose its stability and the confidence of the world. This is already beginning to happen as millions of dollars' worth of gold flow out of this country every month. Few people realize that this is one of the objectives of the Communists—to get us to spend more and more on ourselves until we are financially bankrupt.

. . . The third great problem facing America, of course, is Communism. I have recently returned from the edge of the Iron Curtain. More than five hundred refugees a day crossed over the line from East to West Berlin. I have interviewed some of these refugees, and from the stories they told me, I would rather my children be dead than live under this gigantic anti-Christian system.

There are those who say we should appease the Communists, that they will be understanding and reasonable if we give them more. This is precisely what was said concerning Hitler. More and more was given Hitler, but he was not satisfied until he had plunged the whole world into war. We must conduct a spiritual, ideological, and psychological counteroffensive that will throw back the forces of evil.

"Needed! Strong Men"
The Hour of Decision, 1960

Billy Graham announces another threat which is greater than any external force:

Did you know that the moral problem can threaten the security of America? Our greatest enemy tonight is not Communism; our greatest enemies tonight are not some of these things that we are reading about—our greatest enemy tonight is the immorality in our own country, being taken up with pleasure and materialism and the secularism of our society, the lowering of the moral standards. This will destroy America before Communists ever get to us.

And, of course, there is a plan. The Communists would like to see it continue on the immoral binge because that makes us easy picking. We lose our will to fight for our freedom. We lose our will to resist, and that is what they want.

"The Teen-Age Moral Problem"
Houston Crusade, 1965

Billy Graham solemnly warns that the day of retribution for mankind's sins is not far off:

Ladies and gentlemen, on this warm September afternoon in 1958 I am disturbed by what I see and what I feel. We stand on the brink of catastrophe. Mr. Nehru, speaking to the Indian Parliament, recently said, "We stand on the brink of Hell."

Our leaders are warning us but we have become deaf. Our minds are blinded. Our wills are paralyzed and our consciences dulled.

We are so taken up with our money-making, so taken up with the amusements and places and comforts of modern American life, that we don't realize that the forces of evil are closing in about us. Unless we can turn to God and have His help, we are done for as a nation and a people.

Opening Sermon
Charlotte Crusade, 1958

What a picture of America today—worshiping other gods while giving lip service to the true and living God. I tell you, God is sick of it! I tell you that our false pretenses and our hypocrisy are a stench in the nostrils of God! About the only time some people get on their knees is when they tune their television sets.

"God's Warning"
The Hour of Decision, 1957

America has known times when the national income was much lower. She has known periods in her history when there was less general prosperity than there is now. But America has never known an hour when she faced graver problems than she is facing today. There has never been an hour in our history when we have stood in more dire need of the Presence of God in our national life. With tremendous weapons in the hands of the enemy, with crime and evil continually on the increase, with our moral progress at a standstill, and the embers of faith burning low on the altars of national devotion, we need to cry with voice as a nation, "Let the fire fall!"

"A Religion of Fire"
The Hour of Decision, 1953

America has been given more spiritual and moral light than any nation in the history of the world. We have millions of Bibles at our disposal; there are hundreds of thousands of churches; there are millions of books which explain Christianity. Yet in spite of all this we continue to be the most crime-ridden, the most divorce-prone, and the most immoral nation on earth. Pornography fills our newsstands, and we spew this filth all over the world. When an American Christian travels abroad, he is ashamed to look at the newsstands and see the American magazines. Many of them are filled with crime, sadism, and sex.

How long will God stand by? How long will God withhold his hand of judgment? I tell you it will not be long. The storm clouds of judgment are already gathering on the horizon. Unless we as a nation repent and turn to God, we are going to suffer a judgment such as no nation has ever endured.

"God and the Nations"
The Hour of Decision, 1964

Billy Graham speaks of the feeling of despair which seems to be paralyzing the wills of men throughout the world:

The world in which we live is full of pessimism. We read our current newspapers and news magazines, we listen to the news programs on the radio and watch the television newsreels unfold the tragic drama of a world in the midst of pessimism, frustration, and confusion, and our hearts fail us because of fear. The only light penetrating the darkness, the only hope on the world horizon, is the hope expressed and held out on the pages of the Bible, that Jesus Christ, God's Anointed Son, is some day coming back to this earth. We do not know the time of His coming, but many Christians throughout the world believe it is very near.

"God's 'D-Day' "
The Hour of Decision, 1956

This is what America, this is what Australia and Canada and the world needs! Our nations need a moral bath, but there is only one kind of detergent and that is the blood of Jesus Christ. The tide of evil throughout the nation rushes on unchecked, but a few voices are being raised here and there against it. This country is destined for destruction and judgment as surely as Babylon or Rome were in the ancient world. Our only hope lies in the Cross of Jesus Christ.

"Moral Impurity"
The Hour of Decision, 1959

Billy Graham sees some hopeful signs for America's progress toward rediscovering God:

The whole world is frantically and madly searching for an answer before we blow ourselves to bits. And it's a very wonderful thing that philosophers and scientists and diplomats and political leaders and intellectuals are all beginning to say, "We need God." There is beginning to be an admission on the part of many American leaders that we've lost God somewhere, and that's the first step back to God: when we admit that we've lost him.

. . .

How are we going to get back to God? That's the reason that a lot of people that have reached the top find no peace at the top, they find no joy at the top. They take their tranquilizing pills and their sleeping pills and their Dexedrine tablets and their aspirins slowly in between, because money and fame and fortune have not brought them peace of soul. Why is that? Because you were made in the image of God and without God you can find no peace in this life. Your soul is restless—it cries out for God and you give your soul another sedative. And your soul screams for God: "I'm made in the image of God, I want God." You throw another aspirin in and say, "Be quiet, soul."

Madison Square Garden
New York City
May 15, 1957

Billy Graham finds that many scientists are beginning to discover that simple knowledge is not enough, that greater technology must be equaled by advances in the spiritual realm:

Scientists today have come to the point where they are turning to the Church to help them for an answer. There is nothing but darkness and blackness as the scientist looks out into the future. He sees the possibility of making a wonderful world. Then he looks into the human heart and realizes that the greatest scientific things of our day are building engines of destruction.

Fourteenth Sermon
Charlotte Crusade, 1958

What is needed, says Billy Graham, is a full-scale movement of courageous men and women taking positive action against the forces of sin:

All through history God has called upon men to take courage. The forces of evil are sweeping through our world today. Lust, greed, and hate are manifesting themselves everywhere. Our streets are being turned into asphalt jungles as men rape, mug, rob, and kill. Our world stands on the threshold of a nuclear war that could destroy much of civilization. If ever there was a time we needed men and women to mobilize for Jesus Christ, it is now.

"When Silence Is Yellow"
The Hour of Decision, 1965

Billy Graham discusses a deceptively simple cure for the spiritual disease of sin:

Recently the chairman of one of the most important committees in Congress asked, "Do we need new laws, more streamlined police administration, better law enforcement, heavier sentences, or greater funds to curb crime?" Sociologists, psychologists, and law-enforcement officers alike are wringing their hands over this situation. They seem to have reached the end of the rope. They do not know what the basic cause is, nor do they know the cure. The basic problem is that we are sinners; and the cure is conversion to Jesus Christ. I'm often accused of oversimplifying these problems, but I believe that we've tried the complex answers too long. It is time to get back to the simplicity and the power of the Gospels to transform individuals as well as society.

One of the problems is that the average person feels that the consistent delinquent, the confirmed criminal, or the alcoholic is without hope; so we've often relegated them to the social scrap heap and made little effort to save them. They get lonely, discouraged, and burdened with care just as you and I. Remember that within each person beats a heart just like yours. Sin and lawlessness have rushed in to fill the vacuum. When that void is filled with God, the criminal problem is solved for that person.

"God and Crime"
The Hour of Decision, 1956

CHAPTER V:

SINS AND SINNING

Billy Graham discusses sin as an element inherent in the nature of man:

Personalities are warped by sin; frustration, fears, nervous tension, and a thousand and one other psychological problems have gripped millions of Americans because of this moral disease called "sin."

There are no new sins—only new sinners; there are no new crimes—only new criminals; no new evils—only new evildoers; no new pleasures—only new pleasure-seekers. The Devil has invented no new gimmicks. Sin and its accompanying effects are now and always have been monotonously the same. The murders you read about are no more shocking or no different than the murder of Abel by Cain; the sex perversions, which our modern newspapers play up as daring and new, are only modern copies of the ancient perversions of Sodom and Gomorrah.

After many thousands of years of so-called human progress, education, science, and culture, we are annoyed to discover that man is capable of the same old vices and sins, and that as a race we are spiritually little improved.

"Escape"
The Hour of Decision, 1955

Billy Graham again portrays the innately sinful nature of mankind, but also offers a means of salvation:

There is no doubt that evil in the world is becoming more intensified. Satan is accelerating his activities because he realizes that the time is short. The seeds of evil are propagated from parent to child, with each little one bringing into the world as his spiritual inheritance a propensity for evil which mingles with all his propensities for good. Each new life seems to bring a fresh contribution to the already abundant growth of evil. It is a mere germ at first, expressing itself in rebellion against the mother, the slapping at the father, the tendency toward lying, and the rebellion against all authority on the part of young children.

If early in life the child does not have a personal encounter with the Lord Jesus Christ, then evil sinks its fangs deep into the blood stream and injects its terrifying poison. This poison is active, subtle, swift, and successful.

Its results are catastrophic. It affects the mind, the conscience, and most of all, the will. The mind is blinded, the conscience is deadened, and the will is paralyzed.

However, there is a wonderful cure for this disease. So you today with sin in your heart can be saved by the blood of Christ. Your sins can be washed away. You can have a new nature. You can have Christ actually living in your heart. And it is only as we as individuals come to Jesus Christ that we can make an impact on our society and roll back the tide of evil that seeks to engulf us.

"God and Crime"
The Hour of Decision, 1956

Evil worms its way into our lives by presenting a harmless appearance. What is more beautiful than the full-page, full-color ads of "the man of distinction," dressed impeccably, sipping a glass of whiskey with his friends in the warmth of a well-appointed room? These ads say nothing of the new alcoholics that are being made every day, nor of the growing problem of excessive drinking that is eating at the heart of our civilization. Of course, it wouldn't be good taste to show a picture of a "man of distinction" on skid row, who began his drinking on Fifth Avenue but is ending it in the Bowery. It wouldn't be in good taste, but it would be honest. "Woe unto them that call evil good!"

"Confusing Good with Evil"
The Hour of Decision, 1964

Both the internal and the external effects of immorality are unnatural to behold:

Immorality, which is the sin of perversion and unnaturalness, has a way of making those who harbor it unnatural-appearing. The shifty eyes, the suggestive glance—these are marks of the impure. They are the outward signs of inward impurities. But the outward marks are slight compared to the blemishes which impurity etches upon the soul. Guilt complexes and bad consciences are fashioned in the fires of lustful passion. Out of unbalanced practices of impurity grow phobias which alarm even our most skilled psychiatrists.

"Moral Impurity"
The Hour of Decision, 1959

Billy Graham singles out America's most obvious and prevalent sin:

And I believe tonight that the greatest sin in America is the sin of covetousness.

Americans are considered all over the world as materialistic, worldly, secular, greedy, and covetous.

We are guilty of that sin, as a nation, as a people, and as individuals.

Fourth Sermon
Charlotte Crusade, 1958

The world is not half so impressed by the things that one does not do as they are by the good things that one does. Certainly, one should not do things that are wrong; but there are thousands of people who glory in what they do not do, while they commit more grievous sins by not doing good things. They are guilty of the sin of omission or of negative living.

"The Sin of Omission"
The Hour of Decision, 1955

Billy Graham points out that all sins are not necessarily accomplished through acts:

Exercise judgment as to the books you read, the kind of entertainment you attend, the kind of persons with whom you associate. You should no more allow sinful imaginations to accumulate in your mind and soul than you would let garbage accumulate in your living room.

"America's Immorality"
The Hour of Decision, 1954

Billy Graham clarifies one point of Christian teaching which has led to some confusion:

When you come to know Christ, there dwells within you the Holy Spirit, Who gives you supernatural strength to overcome temptation and evil, so that when you face it, you don't face it alone. The Spirit of God gives you the power to say no.

All of us are tempted. If you have not been tempted, you are the only one in the world. Even Christ was tempted. But the Bible teaches that temptation is not a sin. Many Christians become confused at this point. They are tempted, they think that the temptation is itself a sin, and so they get discouraged and go ahead and sin. But the sin comes only when we yield to the temptation.

"The New Morality"
The Hour of Decision, 1965

The tendency to compromise our values on important moral issues has led to a gradual erosion of America's entire moral structure:

Tolerance, in one sense, implies the compromise of one's convictions, a yielding of ground upon important issues. Overtolerance in moral issues has made us soft, flabby, and devoid of conviction.

We have become tolerant about divorce; we have become tolerant about the use of alcohol; we have become tolerant about delinquency; we have become tolerant about wickedness in high places; we have become tolerant about immorality; we have become tolerant about crime; and we have become tolerant about godlessness.

"The Sin of Tolerance"
The Hour of Decision, 1957

Billy Graham offers these criteria for judging the correctness of any given action:

All right, always ask yourself this question: When it comes to this television program, this radio program, this book, this magazine, this amusement, ask this question: Is it to the glory of God? Can you walk around on the dance floor to the glory of the Lord? "Lord, I'm doing this for your glory." Can you do that? . . . If you can't, you better mark 'er out! It's sin, and it's wrong! . . .

And then . . . ask yourself is the atmosphere good? Is it conducive and healthy to Christian growth? Do I feel stronger spiritually after having been there, or read that, and seen that? "Lord, you know that that burlesque show I saw certainly did give me a lift spiritually." "Oh my, I feel so much closer to the Lord after having read *Forever Amber!*" Can you do that? If you can't, listen to me, if you can't, it's sin in your life! And it's worldly, and it's sinful!

"Youth's Problems"
Dallas, Texas
June 20, 1953

Billy Graham discusses the growing problem of alcoholism:

A man may not be responsible for his last drink, but he certainly was for the first. No disease germ is powerful enough to lead a man to his first drink. Drinking was a sin first, and a disease last.

. . .

Many Christians have been too smug concerning this great and forbidding evil. Negatively they have folded their hands and said, "Drunkenness doesn't bother me," while at the same time they do nothing to "bother drunkenness," and to destroy its devastating power. Christians have often been complacent while such organizations as Alcoholics Anonymous have sprung up to do the job the Church should have been doing all the while.

"Alcoholism"
The Hour of Decision, 1959

This parable conveys Billy Graham's views on gossip and slander:

There is a story of a woman in England who came to her vicar with a troubled conscience. The vicar knew her to be a habitual gossip—she had maligned nearly everyone in the village. "How can I make amends?" she pleaded pitifully.

The vicar said, "If you want to make peace with your conscience, take a bag of goose feathers and drop one on the porch of each one you have slandered." When she had done so, she came back to the vicar and said, "Is that all?" "No," said the wise old minister, "you must go now and gather up every feather and bring them all back to me."

After a long time the woman returned without a single feather. "The wind has blown them all away," she said. "My good woman," said the vicar, "so it is with gossip. Unkind words are easily dropped, but we can never take them back again."

"Things God Hates"
The Hour of Decision, 1955

Another sin of the tongue that is prevalent among Christians is the sin of criticism—going around and trying to take a speck out of our brother's eye when we have a log in our own.

"The Sins of the Tongue"
The Hour of Decision, 1952

Augustine had a motto printed on the wall of his dining room: "He that speaks an evil word of an absent man or woman is not welcome at this table." Would that we had this motto over every table in every home in America.

"Things God Hates"
The Hour of Decision, 1955

. . . Immorality can be commited in the way you dress. If a woman purposely dresses to entice a man to sin, she has committed it whether the act is committed or not.

I heard about a young woman that accepted Christ and one night she was going to a party with her boy friend. She had always dressed to knock the daylights out of the men.

This night as she was putting on one of her dresses, she said she looked into the mirror and it seemed the eyes of Jesus were looking at her.

She said, "I changed my dress and now I dress as though Jesus were my escort every evening."

Wouldn't that be wonderful if all of us acted as though Jesus were our escort every evening?

Fifth Sermon
Charlotte Crusade, 1958

Satan's dream world always ends with disillusionment. Sin, which is his stock and trade, when it is finished brings forth death. There are thousands of people that live in an unreal dream world while shirking their responsibilities toward their family and God. There are thousands of people that read these cheap novels and get a vicarious imaginative thrill out of the experiences they read. There are people that go to the movies, or watch television dramas, or listen to soap operas, and then dream that they themselves are living the same type of lives. The Bible calls this "sin." This can become an evil habit that can rob you of the joy of the Lord.

"Escape"
The Hour of Decision, 1955

Sin pays—but it pays off in remorse, regret, and failure.

"Delusion or Deliverance?"
The Hour of Decision, 1961

CHAPTER VI:

SEX

Billy Graham describes the symptoms and the effects of what appears to be an instinctive sense of sin in modern man:

There are evidences of [a] lost sense of sin in a thousand facets of our modern life. It is evident in the increase of profanity and obscenity. Our depraved speech is a direct reflection of our depraved lives. Our lost sense of sin is evidenced by our accent on pleasure. The hue and cry of today is "Let us eat, drink, and be merry, for tomorrow we die." We are becoming a nation of playboys and are debasing the wisdom God has given us upon the altars of appetite and desire. We are becoming wise to do evil.

Our lost sense of sin is evidenced by our unnatural emphasis upon sex. The sin of impurity does not appear ugly and venomous at first. It comes in the guise of beauty, symmetry, and desirability. There is nothing repulsive about it. Satan clothes his goddess of lust as an angel of love, and her appearance has deceived the strongest of men. God hates this unnatural emphasis on sex in America. It has caused nations to fall. It has over and over ruined the sanctity of the home. It has caused the spiritual downfall of thousands.

"How Wise Is Man"
The Hour of Decision, 1960

Billy Graham discusses "moral impurity" and the so-called "sex revolution" and cautions against the degeneration which is accompanying our lax attitudes toward sexual morals:

The sex revolution that has been taking place, especially in the United States during the last twenty-five years, is changing the lives of men and women more radically than any other revolution in history. This revolution drastically affects the lives of millions, deeply disturbs the community and decisively influences the future of society. Some of our professors of psychology and sociology are teaching that the sex drive is the vital mainstream of human behavior. In the name of science, its fuller satisfaction is urged as a necessary condition of man's health and happiness. Sex inhibitions are viewed as the main source of frustration, mental and physical illness. Sexual chastity is ridiculed as a prudish superstition and marriage loyalty is stigmatized as antiquated hypocrisy.

Immorality and impurity have penetrated almost every area of our American culture. In the realm of literature there is growing preoccupation with the "subsocial sewers." Filthy, pornographic, and obscene books are now on the shelves of most drugstores and newsstands throughout America. Millions of old and young alike are feeding on them every week. The beautiful moral literature of fifty years ago has been displaced by various forms of abnormal, perverse, vulgar, exotic, and even monstrous forms.

The impure influence is also felt in the realm of music. Music has become seductive, sensual, and perverse in the bulk of night-club, television, and radio entertainment.

Many Church leaders are becoming alarmed about the tendency toward sex, filth, dirt, profanity, and even perversion now on the screen in some of the newer films. A recent study disclosed that fifty-five per cent of the topics of modern movies were devoted to sex, and about thirty-five per cent to crime. In fact, a few movies have become so frankly pornographic that they have provoked open protest from various organizations and communities.

"Moral Impurity"
The Hour of Decision, 1959

Many Church leaders now advocate a so-called new morality. What they propose is a standard based on love without law, in which the ultimate criterion for right and wrong is not the command of God, but the individual's subjective perception of what is good for himself and his neighbor in each given situation. In my opinion, this is not a new morality—this is the old immorality.

"The New Morality"
The Hour of Decision, 1965

Billy Graham attacks moral relativism, and admonishes his colleagues to deal openly with the subject of sex for the benefit of the young people:

And during the past years, in our educational systems, we have taught our young people that morals are relative, that they're changeable. We've taught them that there is no such thing as an absolute moral standard and moral code.

We've taught them that they're relative. And Dr. Kinsey said that anything that most of the people are doing must be all right.

In other words, if most of the people are committing adultery and immorality, then it must be accepted as a general practice and it must be all right.

Well, I want to tell you that the Bible has nothing to say about that.

Our young people today know far more about the statistics of Brigitte Bardot than they do about the Seventh Commandment. We've forgotten the Seventh Commandment. We've left it out. Unfortunately, we in the Church, we ministers, have been reluctant to deal about it. Very frankly, I don't like to preach on it. I don't like to talk about it.

But I believe that it's time that some of us in the pulpit deal with this subject of sex that everybody else is dealing with.

The sociologist is dealing with it.

The psychologist is dealing with it.

The psychiatrist is dealing with it.

In our classrooms they're dealing with it.

Advertisers are dealing with it.

Everybody's dealing with it except the Church!

I believe it's time for the Church to speak out and warn our young people that the Bible has a lot to say about it. The Bible doesn't adopt any hush-hush attitude. The Bible talks about it frankly, openly, and straightforwardly.

Fifth Sermon
Charlotte Crusade, 1958

The clergy are trying to teach, and I think many of the clergy across the country are doing all they can by, perhaps, talking about it, but I think we gathered a lot of barnacles on the ship of Christianity. A lot of taboos, a lot of don'ts that really were not taught in the Bible. And we made a hush-hush subject out of this, that, supposed to be dirty if you mentioned it from the platform, and so on. I think the clergy in the country ought to be standing up, telling these young people what the Bible teaches. In no uncertain terms, when I announce in my crusades that I am going to speak on youth, sex, and the Bible, you can't get near the place. Thousands upon thousands of young people are there. They want to hear, and I don't pull any punches. I tell them straight out what the Bible says, that sex outside of marriage is wrong. And the reason God said that is not because God doesn't want you to have a good time. He did it for your own good. Because it has great psychological scars. It affects your marriage in years to come.

And there are many people suffering from mental illness, I think today, and then there are other problems, like the increase in venereal disease, and the increase in abortions, and the one city in this country has twenty drop-outs a day, and it's under a million people. Twenty drop-outs a day from high school girls that are pregnant. You see now, they say the average kid says, "Well, I won't get caught." But thousands are getting caught.

Today
NBC Television
April 19, 1966

Billy Graham cites the Scriptures for his authority on the subject of sex and the marital vows:

Sex is a part of marriage for three things—fulfillment, communication, propagation; and this is to be the communication at the deepest level of marriage. Sex is not just a physical act. God has restricted its expression to the husband-wife relationship, and some of the sins that are the most harshly condemned in the Bible are those involving sex.

They are sins against the eternal purpose of God. God

meant that a man and a woman are to live together until death parts them. They are to remain faithful to each other, and sex outside of marriage is said by the Scriptures to be wrong and sin, and in the Old Testament, God demanded the death penalty for the breaking of the marriage vow.

Now, the Bible also warns against intermarriage. In Exodus 34, Deuteronomy 7, Ezra 9, the people of God were warned against marrying with the heathen and the pagan, those who worshiped other gods, those who did not believe in the true and living God.

You come over to the New Testament, and God has that advice to the young people. If you are Christians, you be sure that the young man you are going with is also Christian. If not, your friendship may deepen into what you think is love, you may marry him, and you are going to end up in serious trouble.

"Problems of the American Home"
Houston Crusade, 1965

Now, every young person in this audience tonight has that problem [sex] because God gave you the gift of sex. There's nothing wrong with it. It is given by God, and the Bible doesn't adopt a "hush-hush" attitude toward it. The Bible speaks plainly about it, and sex in its God-given place can be one of the greatest servants in the world, but it can be a terrible tyrant.

God says that the place for sex is within the marriage. Before marriage, take this gift, dedicate it to God, and it will become a dynamo in your life, that will take you to the top in anything.

"Youth of Today Searching for Security"
Houston Crusade, 1965

The Seventh Commandment plainly says, "Thou Shalt Not Commit Adultery." Nowhere does the Bible teach that sex in itself is a sin. But from Genesis to Revelations the Bible condemns the wrong use of sex. Man in his sinful nature has taken what was intended to be a glorious and complete act of love between two people and has made it something low, cheap, and dirty.

The Bible is one of the world's outspoken books on the subject of sex, and the Bible condemns sex outside the bonds of matrimony. The fact that immorality is rampant throughout the nation doesn't make it right; the fact that some clergyman may condone it doesn't make it right. The Bible says, "There is a way that seemeth right unto a man; but the end thereof are the ways of death" (Proverbs 16:25). Under Jewish law adultery was punishable by death. Under God's law today it also results in spiritual death.

"The New Morality"
The Hour of Decision, 1965

Billy Graham warns against the debasement of the gift of sex and its possible effects upon mankind:

There must be firm control of the sex impulses. This God-given instinct has been dragged through the gutter by modern thinking, and we have made a cheap toy out of one of the most sacred gifts God has ever given to man. Our procreative powers need to be dedicated to Christ. If they are brought under proper control, we can rise to the heights. If they control us, we will sink to the depths.

"Christian Discipline"
The Hour of Decision, 1960

Billy Graham speaks on the subject of sexual morality on America's college campuses:

A growing number of college students do not consider premarital sex immoral. On the contrary, they view it not only as a natural expression of affection, but as a valuable experience in personal growth. The sources of student belief lie in the altered structure of our society, and more deeply in the shift in society's mode of judgment—a shift away from the moral code based on faith in God and toward a code based on psychological consequences.

However, many of our psychologists and psychiatrists are joining some courageous preachers who are speaking out on this subject. They are beginning to say that all this sex freedom is leaving deep psychological problems in thousands of young and old alike.

"America's Immorality"
The Hour of Decision, 1954

We're living today in a period that has been called the American sex revolution, the greatest revolution in the history of the world. Greater than the Communist revolution! And it is said that this revolution will destroy America unless the present trend is reversed.

Our literature, our music, many of our films, even our advertising, have become obsessed with sex.

And so young people are faced with it everywhere.

Now, there's nothing wrong with sex. It's a God-given instinct. And if it's used right, it's a wonderful service. If it's used wrongly, it's a terrible tyrant.

Sex is not moral or immoral—it's amoral.

Third Sermon
Charlotte Crusade, 1958

CHAPTER VII:

INTERNATIONAL STRIFE

Billy Graham points out that the world's apparent pessimism and despair are only the symptoms of a pervasive and persistent human disease:

Today a spell of doom and dismay has settled down upon the hearts of men. No matter where we travel the specter of hopelessness is found. We see it in bold type in the headlines of the papers. We see it in the deep lines that furrow troubled brows. We sense it in man's futile search for fulfillment. We see it in the purposelessness of living. The very atmosphere seems impregnated with a stifling hopelessness that has robbed millions of the zest for living.

Our world is very much like a man who has cancer. When cancer is brought under control in one spot, it often breaks out in another. The world specialists may employ all the diplomacy and skill at their command. They may, as the Bible says, "anoint themselves with the chief ointments," but at best they reach only symptoms, and the cleverest of this world's leaders have failed to diagnose the cause of the disease.

"Spiritual Maturity"
The Hour of Decision, 1959

A firm grasp of history and its implications underlies much of Billy Graham's prophetic vision of the fate of America:

Nazism blossomed in Germany only after the Church had failed to fill the vacuum following World War I. When the Church failed to present and declare a dynamic living Christ, Germany was robbed of a Saviour and gave birth to a dictator. When Christ is made to abdicate from his rightful place as Lord in any nation, tyranny takes over.

"The Risen Christ"
The Hour of Decision, 1964

The failure of our international leaders to come to grips with the heart of the problem is symbolized, for Billy Graham, by the "prayer room" at the United Nations:

It was my privilege to be the guest of the late Dag Hammarskjöld at the United Nations Building in New York. He took me to the little room that has been designated a "prayer room." I went into the semidarkness. There was something missing. Immediately I recognized that there was no cross in that room.

Here was religion without a cross . . . a testimony that the nations of the world are deeply religious but have not yet come to the point where they are willing to accept Christ and Him crucified. Thus the world stumbles blindly on toward eventual judgment and destruction, not realizing that they are rejecting Christ and Him crucified, which is the only possible hope for salvation.

"The Cross and Its Power"
The Hour of Decision, 1958

The leaders of the United Nations organization are blinded to the basic problem of the world. Thus they have no remedy. For centuries men have met, trying to solve the problems of the world in peace councils—the United Nations, the League of Nations, and many other organizations. But they fail because they have never been able to accept the fact that man is basically a spiritual and moral failure. They never recognize the fact that we have sinned and rebelled against God and that our problem is not economic, but educational, not social, but spiritual and theological. Our problem is that we have a disease called sin.

"What Is Wrong?"
The Hour of Decision, 1960

All attempts to deal with the problems of the world in terms of social or economic symptoms must fail:

. . . Karl Marx looked at the problems of the world and said, "Something's wrong." And Karl Marx said that the problem of the world is "social." He said, "You solve the social problems of the world and man will be a happy individual. And we can build a Utopia on earth; we can build a Heaven on earth."

But Jesus said, "You're wrong." He said the problem of the world is not social. The social problems are only symptoms of a deeper problem. The problem of the world is not illiteracy, the fact that millions cannot read and write. The problems of the world are not summed up in poverty.

It's not because there are "have not" nations and "have" nations. It's not social injustice, bad as that may be. The heart of the problem is something deeper, said Jesus. He said our problems originate from within.

And he called it S-I-N, sin—and, ladies and gentlemen, the problem of the world tonight is sin.

Seventh Sermon
Charlotte Crusade, 1958

Because the world system has rejected Christ, it furnishes an ideal sphere for the operation of Satan and his satellite demons. Thus there is no explanation for what is happening throughout the world today, except that it is by the supernatural activity of a powerful but not omnipotent Satan.

"Needed! Strong Men"
The Hour of Decision, 1960

The theoretical source of Communism's rejection of God is outlined by Mr. Graham:

. . . Communist theory displaces all religion, because God, to the Communist, is merely a reflection of man's own necessity; and when man has graduated from the realm of necessity to the realm of freedom, there will be no necessity to be reflected; hence, there is no need of God, says the Communist. In other words, the Communist is promising to build ultimately a new world, but a world without God.

"The Ultimate Weapon"
The Hour of Decision, 1961

The gains which Communism is making all over the world are not the result of any ideological superiority, but rather the result of commitment:

I am convinced that [commitment is] one of the reasons Communism is gaining such momentum throughout the world—and it is—I do not know one place in the world tonight in which Communism is losing.

I do not know one great victory we have won in recent years over Communism. It's gaining slowly but surely, nibbling here and nibbling there, a little bit there, and a little bit here, and coming ever closer to the shores of this country.

The Communist radio in Peiping said yesterday, "War could break out at any moment." Why? Because they're dedicated. They are outdedicating the Christians.

A handful of Communists are winning the world, while 600,000,000 Christians are losing the world. Why? Because they believe in something, and they are ready to die for it. They have an ideology and a philosophy and a religion that they are ready to live for and die for. And we're taking it easy.

Second Sermon
Charlotte Crusade, 1958

The Communists say that time and history are on their side. But they are ignorant of the fact that Jesus Christ is coming to earth again. It is Christ who is in control, and he will determine the outcome.

"Three Keys to Usefulness"
The Hour of Decision, 1962

Billy Graham discusses the role of Christianity in fighting the ideological onslaught of Communism:

By its rejection of orthodox Christianity, the Western world now has no philosophy and no intellectual framework to combat Communism. Thus we see the blindness, floundering, and confusion of our leaders in the face of a disciplined, organized, but atheistic Communism. There is only one philosophical system in the world today that has any possibility of combating the Communist conspiracy, and that is a virile, dynamic, orthodox Christianity.

"The Ultimate Weapon"
The Hour of Decision, 1961

The final answer to the world of difficulties, however, lies not in any philosophy, but in every human being's turning to a more personal relationship with God:

And if every person in America would turn to Jesus Christ right now, our problems would be over tomorrow. Every national and international problem faced by man would be overcome tomorrow if we returned voluntarily to Jesus Christ, every one of them.

"Sin and the Origin of Evil"
Dallas, Texas
June 3, 1953

But, says Billy Graham, regardless of the outcome of the ideological struggle for world domination, no human forces can long remain triumphant on earth:

A lot of people say, "Do you think Communism is going to win the world?" They might win it temporarily but it will be only temporarily, because the Bible says that Jesus Christ is going to establish his Kingdom and the Church shall some day triumph.

Opening Sermon
Charlotte Crusade, 1958

CHAPTER VIII:

THE CHURCH AND EVANGELISM

Billy Graham is well aware of the need for modern clergymen to deal decisively with some of the important social issues of our times:

I think the responsibility of a clergyman on a moral issue, let's say the race question, is quite clear. We know what that answer is. At least, we believe the Bible teaches what the answer is. Now, in the problem, let's say, of Vietnam, we don't know the answer. I mean, I can have my views, you can have yours. Now, the Archbishop of Canterbury made a statement—the present Archbishop of Canterbury, I think he was probably Bishop of Durham at that time, during the Suez crisis. He said conscientious

Christians can take either side of the Suez question. In other words, I find very devout Christians of the United States on both sides of the Vietnam situation. And these are complex problems in which I may have my ideas, and Doctor so-and-so may have his ideas, and they may be contrary one to the other. Now, this doesn't mean that I have less commitment than he does to Christ, or he has less than I do. We just see differently on this. But when it comes to specific moral issues that we can really pinpoint, like the race question, let's say, I think our duty is clear.

Today
NBC Television
April 19, 1966

Billy Graham enumerates the opportunities available to modern evangelists through the mass media:

We have a greater opportunity today than Paul ever had. I imagine if Paul can look down here, he is "champing at the bit." How he would like to be on television! How he would like to have a radio hour! How he would like to get on a plane and go from Corinth to Rome. How he would like to use some of the facilities we have for saving the lost.

Paul isn't here, but we are! God is depending on us.

"The Holy Spirit and Revival in Our Time"
Convention of the National Association of Evangelicals
Chicago, 1952

We can show periods of history where the church condoned many of the great social evils by holding to the status quo, and coming under the pressure of the congregation. And this is absolutely wrong, because if there is any place in the world that a man should feel free to preach the word of God, no matter whom it affects, it's from the pulpit. I mean, he should be a king in the pulpit, and he should speak with authority and power as the great Old Testament prophets did, and as the New Testament apostles did, even though they were put in jail.

. . .

At various times throughout history, the Church has entered the field of trying to wipe out social evil. Perhaps the greatest social upheaval in modern times was in the eighteenth century, when John and Charles Wesley and George Whitfield preached their revivals across Great Britain, and that led to the tremendous social transformation of Great Britain. For example, they did away with child labor. They did all of those tremendous things that we are the recipients of today. And this was largely through preaching the gospel. Now I think that we in the Church today ought to get back to preaching the Bible and the fact that men can be changed through the gospel of Jesus Christ. And in this way we can make our greatest contribution. Secondly, I think that we make our greatest contribution—and the Church is making it today—in its emphasis on the social problems, and throwing a spotlight, being a conscience to the country. Giving moral guidelines to the country. And I think the church has been doing an exceptional job on this in the past few years, especially, now, I think, in the matter of race question. The conscience of the Church was never really lighted until about fifteen years ago, and I think the Supreme Court and other things had to come along to really show the Church its responsiblity in this field.

. . .

Almost till the time of Roosevelt, the war on poverty, what war there was, and there was constantly a war, was carried on largely by the Church. And today most of these things have been taken over by the state, and this is one of the Church's dilemmas at the moment. . . .

I think in our society in which we live, with such a complex society in a growing population, the state has to enter into it. I don't think the Church could possibly do it all. But here's the difficulty: in England, the state has taken it all over, almost. You have protection almost from the cradle to the grave now in some of these countries. But the people have gone away from the Church. Now, the Church has worked for this for years. We have tried to tell the state, your responsibility is in this area. Now the state goes in with everything. And we're finding other problems coming up. Boredom, emptiness, all of these things that are causing psychological problems. So what does man need? The Bible says, Seek first the Kingdom of God and all these things shall be added unto you. And man is a body, he's a mind, but he's also a soul. He's a spirit. And this spiritual part of him needs God. And he's restless till he finds God. And so, if man can have all of these social benefits, he can have these material benefits, fine. But if that's all he has, he's going to end up in total failure. And man needs today, in my opinion, the word of God, he needs an experience with God, he needs to know

God, which I believe he finds through Jesus Christ, and unless he has this, he's going to be restless. He's going to be empty. And that's where I think the Church may be failing today. We in the Church are still emphasizing the material. We ought to be spending our time on this spiritual side. The state's not going to help the spiritual side of man. But we in the Church are given that responsibility.

Today
NBC Television
April 19, 1966

The Church is on the tail end—to our shame!—of progress along racial lives in America today. The Church should be leading instead of following.

"The Holy Spirit and Revival in Our Time"
Convention of the National Association of Evangelicals
Chicago, 1952

Everybody in the Church is for peace. All of us want peace. Everybody wants peace in this nuclear age, but how to achieve peace is not always easy. And you may have peace at the expense of the freedom of millions of people, and there are many moral problems involved here, and I don't think it's just a black and white case. It's a complex problem, and . . . the Church ought to be praying for the President, for the Secretary of State, for the advisors, that God will lead them to make the right decisions.

• • •

The problem of the relationship between the Church and the state has troubled Western nations for many centuries, and is one of Billy Graham's greatest personal concerns:

I think that we in the Church ought to lay down the guidelines for our leaders. Now, we have elected leaders to decide what to do about the political problems around the world. I don't think that I can sit in my home in North Carolina, without all the facts, and make statements about what we should do in these areas. I think we can preach the moral and spiritual guidelines that will help the President, the Secretary of State, and some of these other people to decide, but these people have been elected, and they have the responsibility. And I am not sure that the Church, as a Church, ought to be specifying what to do about certain political situations in the world. I think that we can give general outlines, and moral guidance, but I don't think that we ought to specifically tell them. Now, for example, recently a council met, and they outlined exactly, specifically, what to do about the problems in Asia.

• • •

The difficulty in separating the Church and state, as Billy Graham sees it, arises from the fact that the state has prevented the Church's "interference" but simultaneously forfeited its guidance:

All of these problems you're facing in the job camps today . . . the real problem is we are not giving these men a real motivation. And I think motivation comes from a deep philosophy of life, or it comes from a deep spiritual experience. Now, Mr. Shriver and the men who are running this are doing a wonderful job. This is a great idea, the war on poverty. But man is not just a material being. And I think in America we're in danger of separating [Church and state] so totally that the state can't even mention the word God. Our forefathers never meant that. You can go down to Washington and see God on every building, nearly. The President takes his allegiance of office with his hand on the Bible. The Supreme Court itself is opened with prayer. And when you take prayer out of the schools, and you take the recognition of God out of the schools—and I received a letter the other day from an editor in . . . upstate New York, in which he said a schoolteacher in their town was just teaching rank atheism. He was anti-God, and an evangelist for atheism, but nobody has brought that before the courts, you see. But he can't talk about God and religion, and he can't give moral guidance on the basis of religious experience to these young people. Well, they're going to grow up feeling that there is no such feeling as moral guidelines.

Today
NBC Television
April 19, 1966

We are engaged in this country in a debate on the separation of Church and state. It is important that the Church and state remain separate, but there is another sense in which Christ cannot be separated from anything that pertains to life, for he "is all, and in all" (Colossians 3:11). He said, "Ye call me Master and Lord: and . . . so I am" (John 13:13). He is Master of every phase of our lives.

"The Risen Christ"
The Hour of Decision, 1964

Billy Graham envisions a more dynamic approach to preaching for today's churchmen:

. . . Because I do think that we are living in an era when we need to become somewhat vigorous in our presentation of the gospel to the people. The Communists are. I never saw a Communist orator standing up and giving a dispassionate little lecture. He is usually waving his arms about—and he gets results too.

Evangelical Alliance Address
Westminster, England
May 20, 1952

Evangelism is the fire truck of the Church. When the fire truck comes along, all other vehicles get out of the way, and when the fire truck has done its job, the other vehicles begin to run again.

Press Conference
New York Crusade
Summer, 1957

I'm not here to teach psychology, philosophy, or theology. I'm here to tell what the Bible says. We've listened to the voice of man long enough. Now let's listen to the voice of God!

New York Crusade
Summer, 1957

Billy Graham discusses his own personal role as a preacher of the gospel:

The task as an evangelist is to plant the seed as a farmer would plant seed in the springtime. The farmer cannot make the seed grow, he cannot generate life—this can be done only by God. So when the seed is planted in the human heart, if other conditions are right, God will make the seed grow, causing that person to mature spiritually.

"Spiritual Maturity"
The Hour of Decision, 1959

Addressing a gathering of missionaries, Billy Graham expressed some personal anxiety over the publicity and praise generally lavished upon him:

I want to tell you something I haven't told others on this trip around the world. I feel tonight as if my ministry is going to be very brief. My name has appeared in too many newspapers. It has been placed on too many posters.

There has been too much praise given to a man, and the Bible says God will not share His glory with any man.

Osaka, Japan
1956

Probably it sounds a bit intolerant and narrow to you for an evangelist to go around the planet preaching the Cross—and you are right; for Jesus said that the gate to the Kingdom of Heaven is narrow. But we are narrow also in mathematics and in chemistry. If we weren't narrow in chemistry we would be blowing the place up. We have to be narrow. I am glad that pilots are not so broad-minded that they come into an airport any way they want. Why, then, should we not be narrow when it comes to moral laws and spiritual dimensions?

Harvard Law Forum
Cambridge, Massachusetts
March 26, 1962

Billy Graham cautions against evangelists' using techniques which appeal chiefly to the emotions.

There are several dangers to this business of mass evangelism. The first is the danger of false emotion. I tell you quite frankly that it is possible for an orator to stand up and sweep a mass of people off their feet by his eloquence. It is possible for him to use deathbed tales and moving illustrations, and for people to come forward with great emotion and in tears—and it may look genuine; but the people are weeping over the story told and not over the conviction of sin by the Holy Spirit. I learned this lesson about two or three years ago, and we have cut out all stories and illustrations at the end of our messages, and all emotional stories whatsoever. If you were to come to our meetings, you would say that there is no emotion. You would wonder how anybody made a decision. A man must be convinced intellectually.

Evangelical Alliance Address
Westminster, England
March 20, 1952

CHAPTER IX:

THE WIT OF BILLY GRAHAM

I heard about a man some time ago who had a watermelon patch, and some young rascals in the community were stealing him blind.

So he said, "All right, I'll get 'em." So he put up a sign in his watermelon patch that said, "One of these melons is poison." He went to bed and got up the next morning, and sure enough they hadn't stolen a watermelon. Everything was the same, except the sign had been changed. It now read, "Two of these watermelons is poison."

Ninth Sermon
Charlotte Crusade, 1958

You see, teen-agers have a vocabulary that is all their own, and some of us, if we don't keep up with it, can't understand what they are talking about. Now, I found out that the vocabulary changes about every six months. Things are no longer "cool, dad, cool." Instead they are "out of sight," "fab," "bad," "dyno," "tuff"; that is, up where I live, and the kids don't wear trousers they wear "vives, Italian vives." "Kangaroo shoes" are worn by beatnicks.

And Mom and Dad have become "the old man" and "the old lady" and the telephone is now called "the bell" or "the ring." The Saturday evening party is called "gig," "set," or "grind 'em up," and the twist is now dead, killed by middle-aged women in tight pink stretch pants!

Now it's called the "fish," "dog," "the dirty dog," "the shampoo," "the jerk," "the mashed potato," "the rodent," "the Boston monkey," and "the broken hip." A close friend is a "cut buddy," and a constant companion is a "shadow." A job is called "a hustle" and wages are "green bark" or "bread." But romance is still the central theme, and girls are rated by the boys in our high school as "scabs," "shanks," and "bats."

Now, don't ask me what they mean. I know the "fox" is different. She's a good-looking "dyno," or "out of sight chick." Beatles are the "rock 'n' rollers." The Rolling Stones are "rhythm and blues"; Ray Charles is "pure soul," and Elvis Presley is "an old man still trying."

"Youth of Today Searching for Security"
Houston Crusade, 1965

Throughout his travels, Billy Graham has discovered that there are many ways to overcome the difficulties of language barriers:

You know the young people, teen-agers, have a language all their own. I have three teen-agers in my family and sometimes they speak in a language that I don't quite understand. I've found out that grownups are squares because they can't dig the jive. And I heard about one of these cats who went to church Sunday morning, and when the pastor greeted him at the door he said, "Dad, you really blasted me this morning! That sermon was reet, neat and really sweet! You were on the beam and you were really cool, cool, dad, and I mean but cool."

The minister gulped with astonishment and he said, "I beg your pardon?"

And the teen-ager continued, "Dad, I mean you were on the beam and I was reading you clear. That jive was so hep that I dropped twenty somalies in the plate. Dad, you were great!"

And the minister smiled and said, "Crazy, man, crazy!"

"God's Delinquent"
Recorded Sermon
Great Sermons Series

The Bible warns very strongly that you are to obey your parents. The rod is considered old-fashioned in many homes. Psychiatrists say it will warp your personality. When I did something wrong my mother warped part of me, but it wasn't my personality.

New York Crusade
Summer, 1957

Some of Billy Graham's country upbringing is still reflected in bits of homely but witty wisdom such as this:

A woman once told me all her little boy needed was a pat on the back. I told her if it was low enough and hard enough, it would do him some good.

Pittsburgh Crusade
September 21, 1952

I heard about a father who called his son aside and said, "Son, don't you think it is about time that you and I discussed the facts of life?"

The son said, "I sure do, Dad. What do you want to know?" I think that is the modern young person today!

"The Teen-Age Moral Problem"
Houston Crusade, 1965

What is the diagnosis of Man's disease? We all have a disease. I heard about a man some time ago that graduated from medical school, and he hung his sign up and a patient came to him. And he was an old man and he described all his symptoms, and the young man tried to diagnose it and he failed. And he went back to his inner office, studied all of his med books, and he still couldn't figure it out. He went in and said, "Sir, have you ever had this trouble before?" And the man said, "Why, yes." The young doctor said, "Well, you've got it again."

Madison Square Garden
New York City
May 15, 1957

I remember the first time that I ever went North to hold meetings. I was with a friend of mine who was from Alabama. Neither of us had ever been North before above the Mason and Dixon line, and we stopped at a filling station one day. The man came around and filled up the tank with gasoline and then he asked my friend from Alabama, "How's your oil?"

And my friend from Alabama said, "We s all right, thank you, how's you all?"

Opening Sermon
Charlotte Crusade, 1958

I heard about a man who was supposed to preach for twenty minutes and he spoke for thirty and forty and fifty; an hour and twenty minutes later he was still speaking. The man who introduced him couldn't stand it any longer and he picked up a gavel and threw it at the speaker. It missed the speaker and hit a man in the front row, and as the man in the front row was going into subconsciousness, he said, "Hit me again, I can still hear him."

"Youth of Today Searching for Security."
Houston Crusade, 1965

As a preacher, Billy Graham has had first-hand experience with a peculiar disease which periodically afflicts members of church congregations:

A lot of people get what I call "Sunday-itis" on Sunday mornings. Do you know what Sunday-itis is? It attacks the victim shortly after breakfast on Sunday morning. It is accompanied by a feeling of weakness and lethargy. Sometimes the victim has a slight headache which is aggravated by the ringing of the church bells in the community.

But the disease is of short duration, usually disappearing about noon, when the victim is able to eat a full dinner and play golf in the afternoon.

But the symptoms usually appear again about seven-thirty Sunday evening, and then disappear until the next Sunday morning.

Twenty-ninth Sermon
Charlotte Crusade, 1958

Self-respect is a wonderful thing so long as it is not produced by self-deception. A lady said to her minister, "This morning I stood in front of the mirror for half an hour admiring my beauty. Do you think I committed the sin of pride?" The minister replied, "No, I don't think you committed the sin of pride—it was more the sin of a faulty imagination."

Too often our self-respect is unjustified—it is often a substitute of God-respect.

"The Rivers of Damascus"
The Hour of Decision, 1956

A lady asked me the other day, "Mr. Graham, do you think it's all right for a Christian to wear make-up."

I looked at her and I said, "Lady, you need a little."

Twentieth Sermon
Charlotte Crusade, 1958

Billy Graham comments on New York City's awesome traffic situation:

The only people here are the quick and the dead.

Press Conference
New York Crusade
Summer, 1957

Billy Graham uses this comical story to illustrate the fallacy in a familiar Christian belief:

I saw a man pick up a football once at the Rose Bowl, run sixty-five yards—and 90,000 people cheered; but he ran the wrong way and lost the game. He was the most sincere man I think I have ever seen. I had him right in my field glasses. Boy, he had sincerity on his face as he went down that field. But he was wrong.

Tenth Sermon
Charlotte Crusade, 1958

Billy Graham makes this humorous reference to the long-standing rivalry among the numerous Protestant sects:

I heard about a fellow with a cat sometime ago. He was trying to sell a little kitten. He was taking it up and down the street, and he said "This is a Baptist kitten, a Baptist kitten for sale." And he couldn't sell it. The next day he came around, he said, "It's a Methodist kitten." A man said, "Why, these are the same kittens as yesterday. Why do you call them Methodist kittens?"

"Well, today they've got their eyes open."

Opening Sermon
Charlotte Crusade, 1958

Billy Graham offers this pithy summary of Christian ethics:

A Christian should so live that he would not be afraid to sell the family parrot to the town gossip.

"Three-Dimensional Christianity"
The Hour of Decision, 1955

We've been reading a great deal about Texas in the last few days, and we have some Texans on the platform that are on our team. And those Texans play practical jokes on each other in a big way, as everything in Texas is big. And one of those Texans dropped some sedative in some coffee of another Texan and he went out like a light. They carried him to a newly dug grave in the graveyard. They put him in the grave and left him there in the coffin. The next morning he awakened. He felt the satin in the coffin. He looked all around, wondered where he was, stood up, looked out over the grave and saw the tombstone. And then all of a sudden he gave an exclamation. He gave a shout. He said, "Hallelujah, it's Resurrection Morning and a Texan is the first up."

Madison Square Garden
New York City
May 15, 1957

Billy Graham is an outstanding man of God, but he is also a devotee of the game of golf, and, as this anecdote proves, a golfer is a golfer:

I played golf today with Bishop Harmon of the Methodist church and Dr. Jack Huneycott, pastor of Hawthorne Lane Methodist, and modesty forbids me announcing who won the game. I win so seldom that when I do, I have to announce it.

Now the bishop was very interested in theology and we had a theological study all the way around. Just before he would go to hit the ball, I would ask him another question. He would get his mind on it, and he could not hit the ball. We worked that idea on Grady Wilson for a number of years and it always works! Golf is a game of concentration.

Sixteenth Sermon
Charlotte Crusade, 1958

I heard about one preacher one day, and he was preaching, and he said, "Has anybody ever heard of a perfect man?" He didn't expect anybody to stand up. Finally there was one spineless little fellow stood up in the back —little, weak, weasel-faced fellow. And he stood up sort of hesitatingly. And the preacher said, "You know of a perfect man?"

And he said, "Uh, yes, sir, I do."

And he said, "Well, who?"

And he said, "Well, my wife's first husband was perfect."

"Problems of the American Home"
Dallas, Texas
June 23, 1951

I was coming down on an elevator with some friends of mine and a man got on about the fifth floor and he said, "I hear Billy Graham is on this elevator," and one of my friends pointed in my direction and said, "Yes, there he is."

The man looked me up and down for about thirty seconds and he said, "My, what an anticlimax."

"Why God Allows Suffering and War"
Houston Crusade, 1965

Ringling Brothers Circus has been called the greatest show on earth, but I think when the history of our times has been written, they will say that an American political convention is the greatest show on earth.

"Emotion"
The Hour of Decision, 1956

Teen-agers today also have too much leisure time. That was never a question in my day. I got up at three A.M. to milk the cows, and when I got out of school I had to milk the same cows. Somehow they had filled up again.

New York Crusade
Summer, 1957

Billy Graham's sarcasm cuts right to the heart of the contemporary attitudes toward worship and religion:

You don't want too much religion. One fellow told me the reason he likes his church is because there is no mention of politics or religion. That is a fact, he really told me that. I will not tell you what denomination; I would be ashamed to tell you.

Oh yes, go to church; it doesn't disturb, it doesn't cost you anything. Oh, you throw in maybe a dollar in the collection, or you flip the Lord a fifty-cent piece on Sunday. You throw a little tip to the Lord and say, "Here you are, Lord. I'll tip you."

Twenty-second Sermon
Charlotte Crusade, 1958

Many years ago an Englishman was visiting down here in Texas. They showed him everything—they showed him the skyline in Dallas, they brought him to Houston, into San Antonio, they took him all over Texas, and when he finished touring Texas, they said "What do you think of Texas?" He said, "Well, it is the most fantastic state I've ever been in. You have got everything but one thing."

They looked at him and said, "What do we not have?" He said, "You don't have culture." The old Texan reached in his pocket and said, "How much will that cost?"

That's the way we Christians are. We'd rather just pay for it than have to live it every day. How much would I have to give to the university or the church in order to get into Heaven?

"The World on Fire"
Houston Crusade, 1965

There are a lot of people who have an idea they're going to get up to Heaven and come up to the gate and say to St. Peter, "How much is it going to cost me?" And then you'll pull out a five-dollar bill and you say, "Will that cover it?" And slap it down!

"The Greatest Sin in Dallas"
Dallas, Texas
June 26, 1953

The world says that all we need to do is be decent, respectable, and reasonable. True, that is all one needs to do to be a member of the Great Society, but to be a member of the Kingdom of God, there must be an inner change.

A Communist in Hyde Park, London, pointed to a tramp and said, "Communism will put a new suit on that man."

A Christian standing nearby said, "Yes, but Christ will put a new man in that suit!"

"The Kingdom Society"
The Hour of Decision, 1965

Preaching in a large sports stadium can have both advantages and disadvantages, as Billy Graham noted in Houston:

Now, you know these seats are made for baseball and football, but for a preaching service they are too comfortable, too many people can go to sleep.

I like those old hard wooden benches, where you twist and turn and you stay awake, and you get your calisthenics while listening to the preacher.

"The World On Fire"
Houston Crusade, 1965

Billy Graham discusses the techniques of public oratory:

And when you learn to speak, learn to breathe from your diaphragm. Don't ever speak from your throat. You don't speak from your throat, you speak from your diaphragm. Learn to breathe properly, learn to drink properly (I mean water), and you'll be a good speaker.

"Faith"
Dallas, Texas
June 10, 1953

Billy Graham offers this characterization of modern churchgoers:

We are guilty of spiritual lethargy. Sometimes we sit about like overstuffed toads and we croak and grunt at the right place with a sleepy "Amen" and a weak "Hallelujah." Once in a while you can get us to jump, but not very often.

"The Holy Spirit and Revival in Our Time"
Convention of the National Association of Evangelicals
Chicago, 1952

I've been married for ten years. I want to tell you I love my wife ten million times more than I did the night I married her. I really do, and we're sweethearts still. Boy, I want to tell you—I'd better not get started on that. I remember the first time I ever kissed her; I guess I've kissed her about ten billion times. It's a wonder she has any lips left, or I have any, and I wish she were here tonight.

"Youth's Problems"
Dallas, Texas
June 20, 1953

Well, I heard about a man who had read a book review on Bridie Murphy and the transmigration of souls. He was helping his wife with the dishes and he asked his wife, "Does that mean if I die I will come back to this world in another form?"

"Yes, that's what it means," his wife said.

"Do you believe if I were to die, for example, I would come back as a worm?"

"Sweetheart," she replied, "you are never the same twice."

Twenty-second Sermon
Charlotte Crusade, 1958

Today you are not socially prominent in the business world unless you have an ulcer! Yet ulcers are caused by anxiety, worry, and fear. A famous doctor said sometime ago that the condition of stomach ulcers goes up and down with the stock market.

"The Holy Spirit and Revival in Our Time"
Convention of the National Association of Evangelicals
Chicago, 1952

And get a Bible with big print. I think one of the greatest tricks the Devil ever pulled off on the American people was when he started printing Bibles with such little print that nobody can read them, especially we that are getting old and have bifocal trouble.

Madison Square Garden
New York City
May 15, 1957

Samson was very handsome—the girls were attracted to him. And Samson was very strong. You know what he did? One day he was out in a field, and a lion came, roared and sprang at him, and Samson turned around and took the lion's jaws in his bare hands and ripped his head open. Now, that takes a pretty good man to do that. Tarzan couldn't even do that—he had to have a knife!

"God's Delinquent"
Recorded Sermon
Great Sermons Series

I heard about a fellow sometime ago who was talking to a friend of his and he said, "Boy, my wife is an angel."

The friend said, "You're lucky, my wife is still living."

Twenty-second Sermon
Charlotte Crusade, 1958

The smallest package I ever saw was a man wrapped up wholly in himself.

"Escape"
The Hour of Decision, 1955

ABOUT THE AUTHORS

BILLY GRAHAM—evangelist, author, educator—was born in Charlotte, N.C., in 1918. An ordained Baptist minister, he is the founder and president of The Billy Graham Evangelistic Association, with headquarters in Minneapolis, Minnesota. His extensive personal crusades have taken him to nearly every state in the Union and to many foreign countries. He is also the leader of the weekly *Hour of Decision* TV and radio programs. When he is not traveling he lives in Montreat, N.C., with his wife, Ruth. The Grahams have three daughters and two sons.

BILL ADLER is the editor of *The Kennedy Wit, The Churchill Wit, The Stevenson Wit,* and many other successful books.